The Use of Groups in Social Work Practice

Bernard Davies
Department of Applied Social Studies
University of Warwick

Routledge & Kegan Paul

London and Boston

First published in 1975
by Routledge & Kegan Paul Ltd
Broadway House, 68-74 Carter Lane,
London EC4V 5EL and
9 Park Street,
Boston, Mass. 02108, USA
Set in ten point Pilgrim on eleven point body
and printed in Great Britain by
Northumberland Press Limited, Gateshead

ISBN 0 7100 8085 9 (c)
     0 7100 8086 7 (p)

General editor's introduction

The Library of Social Work was originally designed to make a contribution to the recent significant expansion in social work education. Not only were increasing numbers of students training for social work, but the changing demands of the work and widening view of its theoretical bases were producing considerable changes in the basic curriculum of social work education. In this situation a library of short texts intended to introduce a subject, to assess its relevance for social work, and to guide further reading had a distinctive contribution to make. The continuing success of the Library of Social Work shows that this contribution is still highly valued.

The Library of Social Work will, therefore, continue to produce short introductory texts, but it will also enlarge its range to include the longer, more sustained treatment of subjects relevant to social work. Monographs reporting research, collections of papers, the more detailed and substantial explanation of the knowledge base of social work, could all be encompassed within this wider definition of the scope of the Library of Social Work.

The present work is the second volume in the Library devoted to exploring the use of groups in social work. Like the earlier work by McCullough and Ely, this is directed at social workers 'deeply imbued with the spirit and attitudes of casework' who are 'entering often complex interpersonal encounters'. It seeks to 'encourage caseworkers to use groups as an integral part of their professional practice' and assumes, like McCullough and Ely, that 'no one book could entirely meet this need'. Unlike the earlier work, however, the present book adopts an interactionist approach. Obviously, to some extent, books on 'groups' will contain some overlapping material, but the re-working of such material from a different perspective provides insights and further questions that social work cannot afford to neglect. One of the early objectives of the Library was to provide the opportunity for just this re-working.

This book has a welcome place in the Library of Social Work because it sees that understanding and action in group situations is something far wider than skill in intervention in what Bernard Davis calls 'set-piece' group work. The author draws important conclusions from this approach for thinking about social work method, training and recruiting.

Contents

General editor's introduction   *page* v

Acknowledgments   ix

1   The professional context of group work   1
    Origins and underlying assumptions of this book   1
    An 'interactionist' perspective   2
    An 'internal' frame of reference   3
    The meaning of group work and its settings   6
    The concept of 'client' in an interactional framework   8

2   Group work in the British social work tradition   10
    Groups as a helping medium   10
    Groups in social work   11
    The casework tradition   12
    The North American experience   15
    Future needs in Britain   17

3   What is 'a group'?   20
    Problems of defining 'a group'   20
    A working definition of 'group'   22
    The definition in practice   25

4   Why use groups?   30
    Group work and social work's strategic purposes   30
    Individualising the group member   31
    Some general advantages of group work   33
    Tactical goals for group work   42
    The caseworker's underlying bias   48
    A special problem of group work: confidentiality   49
    The limitations of group work   54

5 The processes of interaction   57
   The self as a social product   57
   An interactionist perspective in practice   60
   The 'organisation' of group interaction   62
   Formal and informal elements of group organisation   68
   Stages of group development   70
   The emotional content of group interaction   82

6 Group tasks and their impact   84
   A group and its tasks   84
   Social work criteria for evaluating group activity   86
   What do activities do to people?   89
   The ingredients of group activity   92
   Analysing activities: its limitations and uses   102

7 The worker inside and outside the group   104
   The group worker's role: fantasy and reality   104
   The authority of the group worker   107
   The worker outside the group   109
   Targets for intervention within the group   118

8 The future for group work   131
   Some key assumptions   131
   Conclusion   140

   Suggestions for further reading   143
   Bibliography   145

Acknowledgments

This book could not have been written without the stimulation and challenge I have received over the years from practising social workers, social-work and youth-work teachers, and students. I need particularly to thank those officers in the Northern Region of the Probation and After-care Service in England, who, during in-service courses, fed so much lively and relevant practical experience into our dialogue on group work. They, their regional training officer Bill Bayley, and my fellow tutors on some of those courses, Tom Carroll and Peter Clason, provided priceless opportunities for me to understand better what *I* had experienced in groups and to develop the theoretical basis of my own work.

I want also to thank the colleagues, friends and members of my family who read all, or parts of, the various typescripts of this book, and especially Ina Clason for actually producing the type-scripts in such an efficient and accurate way.

Note

None of the case-material used in this book refers to actual situations. Though made as realistic as possible, it has been composed especially for the book.

I
The professional context of group work

Origins and underlying assumptions of this book

In the immediate future, more and more social workers are likely to find themselves practising in group situations, whether willingly or through force of circumstances. The 1969 Children and Young Persons Act and the 1972 Criminal Justice Act have brought intermediate treatment schemes, day treatment centres and community service orders, all of which could impose on social workers a great variety of group contact with clients. (See, for example, Aplin and Bamber, 1973, and Thorpe, 1973.) Other legislation, as well as some major new central- and local-government initiatives—reorganised social services departments with a greater community orientation, various urban aid schemes, community development projects and so on—are having a similar, if less direct, effect.

As a result, social workers deeply imbued with the spirit and attitudes of casework are entering often complex interpersonal encounters. A clear need thus exists for literature on group work which arises out of, and draws specifically on, some of this British experience. It must unreservedly seek to encourage caseworkers to use groups as an integral part of their professional practice, and to do so more deliberately, more rigorously and with more knowledge than they might do if just left to their own intuitions. No one book could entirely meet this need, of course, and this one makes no such claim. What follows is intended only as one possible offering, incomplete, and open to continuing dialogue and debate.

This book arises directly out of the needs and demands of caseworkers, as expressed on a variety of in-service courses on group work held between 1967 and 1974. These courses—attended by well over 100 professional social workers who had been trained and were practising as caseworkers—were mounted because the participants, by their own admission, wanted to understand how they might operate or operate more effectively in groups. For them, the key questions were immediate and pragmatic: What is a group? How dangerous is it? Why am I so fearful of working within it? How might it be constituted? How big should it be? What should it be for? What should it do? How is it different from the one-to-one human encounter? And so on.

Because the starting-point of these courses was so pragmatic, many of the philosophical questions which underlie this type of practice were hardly ever posed, still less confronted. And this avoidance has undoubtedly persisted into this book. In particular, it has been taken for granted that social work practice which focuses on the *interpersonal* dynamics of human activity is justified and can have worthwhile results. Such a starting-point, of course, ignores some of the currently fashionable issues with which social work is preoccupied. It does not explicitly take into account, for example, the need for social workers to intervene at the structural (and especially the economic and political) levels of society's functioning. It does not examine the tendency of social workers to manipulate individuals and their interpersonal exchanges in order to control them on behalf of that society. And it does not question the assumption that social workers, by definition, have special insights into, and therefore should exercise great power over, their clients' lives.

These questions are held in abeyance, not because they are regarded as unimportant but because the most pressing need at the moment seems to be to respond to social workers as they are. Their demand apparently is that, as group work roles are thrust upon them, they be provided with some immediate and practical help.

An 'interactionist' perspective

And yet, in spite of these limited objectives and perspectives, this book does involve a good deal of questioning of the conventional social work stance. It must, of course, do so by definition, since, by focusing specifically on a method which in social work is still the exception rather than the rule, it inevitably challenges the pre-eminence of the one-to-one interview within social work thinking and practice generally.

However, quite deliberately, this questioning of conventional social work goes much further. For, in the first place, a book about group work must inevitably give a high priority to relationships *among clients* as well as to those existing between workers and clients. This emphasis on client interaction—and especially on client interaction here and now in group situations—means that

2

(comparatively speaking) very little explicit attention is paid to psycho-analytic theory. This latter is certainly not scorned or rejected as valueless. But, for a social worker practising as a group worker in many contemporary British settings, it is regarded as often of less immediate usefulness than alternative, social psychological perspectives. Thus, this book focuses primarily on individuals' interactions as they are *currently* experienced, and very much less on the emotional and attitudinal residue of *past* experiences and events. The current images and expectations which individuals have of themselves and of others, thus receive considerable scrutiny, with the self-presentations and the resulting patterned relationships being treated as the main materials with, and through which, a group worker might work.

As a corollary of this, the approaches emphasised are not primarily concerned with the direct manipulation of an individual's inner feelings and intra-psychic processes, in so far as this is ever possible anyway. Rather, the issues which are throughout treated as central are: How might a worker help a group to develop its *acknowledged* tasks and agendas—its discussion, clay-modelling, rock-climbing or whatever—and its *current* interactions? How might he or she help the individuals involved to derive a more satisfying experience from these exchanges? and How might these exchanges enable group members to lead more fulfilled and autonomous lives outside the group?

An 'internal' frame of reference

A further, and major, break with much conventional social work concerns *the worker's* perspectives. These, it is assumed, like the knowledge, insights, and interpretations on which they rest, can by no means be regarded as the only ones which are valid or potentially helpful in interactional situations. The client's point of view—the highly subjective meaning *for him* of his current experience—must also be regarded as critical in the relationships and events of which he is part. For, what people do may repeatedly follow very directly from how, at this moment, *they* define their situation and its realities. This definition may or may not be 'accurate' when measured by the objective criteria of relatively uninvolved outsiders like social workers. In itself, however, this does not invalidate it or render it irrelevant.

Indeed, in this book, this 'phenomenological' frame of reference is applied wherever possible. Basic to it is the assumption that (Combs *et al.*, 1971, p. 82):

The person's private world cannot be directly invaded or manipulated. No matter how strongly it may be bombarded from without, the feelings, attitudes, ideas and convictions of which it is composed remain forever the sovereign possession of the person himself. For the person who holds them, meanings are the facts of life. A fact is not what is : a fact for any person is what he believes is so.

The need for such a perspective is becoming increasingly clear. (See for example, Mayer and Timms, 1970.)

Yet, this 'internal frame of reference'—this emphasis on events as seen and experienced by those taking part in them, and on responses to those events according to the participants' own subjective meanings and perspective, has not by any means always been a high priority in social work. Indeed, 'helpers' have often been intent on fashioning meanings for events out of their own perceptions, using criteria of what is significant and tools of analysis which are useful to *them*.

Moreover, because such analysts have been inclined to see an individual's behaviour as the product of forces at work within him (for example, unconscious motivation), they have in effect defined the individual as a mainly unresponsive object. His highly subjective responses to, and interpretations of, what he is experiencing —the meaning of events *for him*—have thus often been treated as having no special relevance for what he does subsequently. They apparently have no significant feedback effect on the events themselves.

Clearly, the position of the non-involved analyst can never be avoided altogether. The worker is not the client, and can never fully get inside the latter's experience. Nor can he ever fully understand or act on the meaning the client attaches to what is happening. Moreover, a relatively detached perspective can at times be immensely helpful, not least to a group worker. All behaviour can have meanings over and above what is revealed or felt directly by the actor. The residue of earlier experiences—of people and relationships and of the feelings, attitudes and responses associated with them—do of course echo again and again in later life. Yet they may be barely available, and seem hardly significant, to the individual concerned. The work and influence of Bion (1961), for example, shows how meaningful and acceptable this particular perspective can be to many who play helping roles in groups, and to those they help.

Nonetheless, such a frame of reference does—at least by implication—tend to see the individual in any interaction as an object,

almost a victim, who in the present is being acted upon by unconscious forces which come from deep within himself. And it also
tends to define the client's perspective as 'fantasy' or 'distortion'
or 'defensiveness' or 'resistance', and again by implication, compare
it unfavourably with the worker's 'reality' point of view. It seems
to attach remarkably little importance to the way the actors themselves, currently and consciously, experience—that is, receive, interpret and judge—the people and events of their group life.

Seeing *and accepting* the world (as far as possible) as the client
sees and understands it *now* may at times be crucial, therefore,
especially for the group worker. It may highlight that, for *group
members*, influential and valuable elements of 'reality' reside in
their current interactions with others. Far from being passive
objects, they are, by definition, actors who constantly feed back
into this network of group exchanges. Thus, not only are they
responding to the interaction around them; they are also, in doing
so, helping to create and re-create that interaction, and especially
the specific form in which it is carried on. The highly subjective
meanings which each individual group member attaches to his
group experiences, helps repeatedly, even if only partially, to
remake the world around him in his own image.

Thus, a phenomenological stance must modify the traditional
social work assumption that the social worker alone observes with
discrimination what the client's situation is—that is, 'diagnoses'
the 'need'. And it must also challenge the conventional view that
the social worker alone 'intervenes' in order, himself, to 'treat' the
client's social and psychological maladies. In what follows, this
framework is by no means abandoned completely. Indeed, very
heavy reliance is at times placed on it—for example in the discussion in Chapter 6 of Robert Vinter's analysis (1967b) of group tasks
and the social worker's control of these. However, in this book,
alternative perspectives do get considerable attention. In particular,
much greater stress is given to the *interactional* processes so
central to group work, and to the impact of client meanings and
interpretations on these processes. That is why, as well as the
work of Vinter, the contrasting, and even at times conflicting,
influence of William Schwartz (1971) has been acknowledged. For
what Schwartz highlights is not 'diagnosis' but 'contract'—that is, the
agreement (formal or informal) between worker and client on what
are viable and acceptable ends and content for their work together.
And what therefore he stresses, as the worker's contribution to
the helping process, is less 'treatment' than 'mediation'—between,
for example, group and agency, and between a group and its wider
environment. Thus, Schwartz's focus throughout is on collaborative

5

activity between worker and client, rather than on largely worker-defined and worker-controlled operations.

These clearly are vitally important concepts for group work. As this book will emphasise repeatedly, one of the key advantages of group experience for social work clients is the opportunity it offers them to play new roles, including 'helping' as well as 'helped' roles. Clients, in other words, have the chance to do unto other clients as the worker would do unto them, or perhaps as they would have him do unto them. The worker's intervention, in order to 'diagnose' and 'treat', is, then, by no means necessarily the only significant intervention which may occur. Reciprocated 'helping' intervention by clients themselves, according to *their* definitions of the realities of the situation, makes a focus on 'contract', 'mediation' and 'collaborative activity' both logical and necessary.

The meaning of group work and its settings

However, in its definition of 'group work', this book attempts to extend the social worker's perspectives even further. For, at times, it takes a very broad view indeed of how the term might be applied as well as of the settings in which groups might be used. Certainly, it accepts that 'discussion groups' do, and will continue to, have a significant part to play in social work practice. However, it certainly does not assume that group work for the social worker is synonymous with discussion group work, no matter how intensive or intra-psychically probing this may be. 'Activity groups' are most definitely seen also as legitimate arenas for social work practice, meriting an informed and disciplined approach. Such groups might work on clearly defined, and partially or wholly formalised tasks: they might rock-climb, sew, do community service and so on. Or they might have the much looser formation and content found, for example, in the 'social clubs' in which adolescents, unsupported mothers, the old, the handicapped and many others increasingly meet under social work auspices. Throughout, however, their non-verbal as well as verbal exchanges are treated as potentially significant channels for providing social work help.

Or again, groups specially sponsored and created by social workers are assumed often to contribute valuable services to social work clients. Nonetheless, much of what follows might be applied —indeed, is explicitly related—to 'natural' groups. This means that the book may be seen as relevant to youth work (including 'detached' youth work, where more intensive contacts with smaller groups are usually possible). And it may also apply to a great deal that goes by the name of community work, and in particular much that is now done with small action groups, planning and protest groups and the committees of voluntary and self-help associations. In all these settings, the 'contract' with those served may often be different from that which binds, say, probation officers or social service department personnel. As implied earlier, a joint agreement may have to be reached between social worker and clients which reflects, much more fully than in 'traditional' social work settings, the clients' definition of the helping situation, its objectives and its rules of operation. Nonetheless, this will not reduce, and may even increase, the worker's obligation to operate sensitively and constructively within quite complex interpersonal exchanges.

Indeed, at this point, it is probably beginning to emerge that, in this book, group work is defined in a very extensive way indeed. On many occasions, for reasons of convenience or simplicity in presentation, the focus will in fact be on 'set piece' groups—groups operating within quite clear-cut boundaries of place, time, membership and task. And yet, one overall intention of this book is to broaden social workers' conceptions of 'group' beyond this rather limiting one, and to suggest that 'group work' need not just mean work in formalised group situations. The starting-point for 'group work' does not have to be imposed by a particular agency, its policies and the limitations these create. Rather, the crucial factor about 'a group' might be—indeed, in this book is repeatedly assumed to be—those processes and structures which inevitably emerge (however primitively) when, *whatever the setting*, three or more human beings begin to exchange words, actions and feelings. It is the existence of this exchange—of this interaction—which is seen as constituting 'a group situation'. The formality or otherwise of the tasks, roles, relationships and institutional framework are regarded as particularising this situation, but not as removing or changing certain common, and key, elements of it.

'Group work' in this context is therefore defined as that element of social work which goes on within, and through, interactional processes and structures. In addition, however, it is defined as that work which is to some degree deliberately designed and self-consciously carried out. For, in a social work context, the intention must be to influence and harness the processes and structures so that they serve ends accepted as 'good' and 'permissible' by the social work profession. The responsibility to pass often self-conscious judgments and to adhere to stated value positions is thus never denied. What is also emphasised, however, is the worker's understanding and activity *vis à vis* the current human *interactions* in which he is directly involved, and through which he attempts to achieve his vocational ends.

7

The concept of 'client' in an interactional framework

These, then, are some of the revisions to a traditional social work framework and perspective, which a book on group work encourages:

1. A focus on social psychological rather than on purely psycho-analytical sources of understanding

2. An acknowledgment of the importance of practical and non-verbal, as well as on primarily verbal, intra-psychically oriented, tasks

3. An 'internal' (phenomenological), rather than a purely 'external', perspective on clients, events and the 'reality' attaching to these

4. Group-centred, rather than mainly work-centred, sources and channels of help

5. A re-interpretation of a great many 'ordinary', 'everyday' working relationships and exchanges as 'group' situations because of their 'interactional' context and significance

This degree of revision implies other, more specific, modifications of the traditional framework, which are not always easy to implement in practice. It casts doubt, for example, on the very use of the term 'client' to describe the person whom social work activity is meant to help. For the term conveniently reinforces the conventional conception of social work, in which the helper has most of the insight and power and so is in the dominant position, while the person helped is regarded as having much less relevant or valid understanding of his plight and so is inevitably seen as inferior and as in the position of supplicant.

As we shall see later, this process of labelling individuals can, in any interactional situation, do much to pre-determine the behaviour of those individuals in the situation. It moulds many of the images and expectations which they have of themselves and which others have of them, and so can quite rigidly pattern the relationships which result. Thus, some of the participants are likely to begin actually to perform according to their label—in this case, as clients. They may then come to see themselves, and to act, as inferior beings who are highly dependent on social workers, not only for practical services, but for very definitions of their troubles and even of their 'personalities'.

Yet, in practice, it is not easy to drop the term, because an acceptable shorthand alternative does not come easily to hand. And so, throughout this book, the term 'client' is retained. Moreover, this could be taken as symptomatic of much else that follows. Points of view are retained, not because they are completely

8

adequate or because their inadequacies have not been recognised; they are retained because, as yet, no satisfactory alternatives seem to have been defined—or, put in another way, because social work theory in general is as yet so primitive and undeveloped.

The book is therefore pragmatic and eclectic, drawing on a wide variety of sources of understanding which seem of use in practice, but which together often suggest contradictions. It represents the author's thinking and analysis at a particular moment in time, and is not intended as a definitive statement, for him or anyone else, of what the use of groups in social work practice might involve. It is in effect one frame removed somewhat arbitrarily from a constantly moving film. The justification for reproducing and printing this snapshot is that it might provide just a little more illumination for some, at least, of those many social workers who are now operating in interactional situations, and whose thinking and practice is now also on the move.

2
Group work in the British
social work tradition

Groups as a helping medium

Varieties of group work are now well established in many fields of
British human relations practice. Agencies whose purposes are
primarily educational or recreational often work through groups.
In many primary schools, for example, children's family or friendship or classroom groupings are quite deliberately preserved within
the classroom, and exploited for the sake of learning. (See, for
example, Grainger, 1970; Kaye and Rogers, 1968; and Richardson,
1967.) So, too, in most youth organisations, are the peer groupings
of teenagers, whether these are 'natural' or deliberately formed for
a specific activity or purpose (see Matthews, 1966). Much of what
goes on in community centres and old people's clubs may be based
on work with groups. Moreover, the use of groups in these settings
is frequently sufficiently self-conscious and disciplined to justify
the title 'group work', in the sense in which this term is used in
this book.

Psychiatric hospitals and other institutions concerned with
mental illness also often use group relationships (see Foulkes and
Anthony, 1965). Indeed, the 'free' and 'unstructured' group sessions,
in which patients are encouraged to talk and act out their feelings
quite uninhibitedly, seem to be better known to many social
workers than other forms of group work. Whether this 'knowledge'
is based on fact or fantasy about the frequency or content of each
session is not, however, always clear.

Industrialists, too, have become devotees of group work, in
the sense that they frequently wish to take into account, and to
exploit, the group formations that occur on the shop-floor or in
the office (see Argyle, 1972a, 1972b; Brown, 1954). No doubt, their
intention is, at least in part, to benefit the workers concerned in
some personal way. Ultimately one can only suppose that this

deliberate intervention in workers' group experience is also seen as a way of increasing output, and profits. This in itself does not mean, however, that what is being done is not 'group work'.

In addition, training for these different areas of work has increasingly, in recent years, come to rely on a careful use of group experience (Rice, 1965; Button, 1971; Abercrombie, 1960; Somers, 1968). Thus, a large number of 'practitioners with people', who professionally have a great deal to gain or lose, apparently believe that group work can help them to achieve their professional objectives.

Groups in social work

To some degree, social workers, too, now share this belief. Certainly, they have at times worked through groups and group situations, even if their use of these has been largely intuitive. There is, for example, the long-standing tradition of social work to be found in the settlements, where formal and informal group meetings have often played a vital part. Much residential work—in community homes, probation and prison after-care hostels and so on—also throws up group encounters which, often in very informal—even casual—ways, are used by social workers. And some youth work carried on primarily for remedial or therapeutic purposes might also be said to fall into this category. (See Goetschius and Tash, 1967; Smith, Farrant and Marchant, 1972.)

A substantial amount of social work is, of course, also carried on with families. (See Jordan, 1972.) Much of what has been done has been seen as a straight extension of casework, and analysed and practised as such. If it has been considered as group work, few of the insights—and certainly few of the social psychological insights—now emerging from the study of groups in general seem to have been systematically applied. Only slowly, it would seem, is the family coming to be dealt with by social workers as a dynamic entity which creates its own distinctive role expectations, performances, conflicts, sanctions and so on.

More recently, however, social workers have begun deliberately to form groups, or to move into existing group situations in order to influence their development and activities in 'desirable' ways. The effects of new legislation, and the current searching criticisms of 'conventional' social work, were both mentioned in the last chapter. There have also been other pressures and professional disappointments; for example, the obvious ineffectiveness of case-work with certain clients (such as with some working class adolescents—see M. Davies, 1969—ex-prisoners, and by overburdened mothers with young children) as well as the attendant upsurge of interest in community work. Any such pressure on social workers to move away from methods focused on one-to-one, office-based treatment with a psycho-therapeutic bias seems bound in the longer term to increase their use of group approaches.

Thus group work has gradually become more fashionable among social workers—almost, it would seem, a fad. Indeed, at times, their acceptance of the method has, if anything, been rather too pat. Often quite consciously, they have allowed themselves to be influenced by just one form of group work, which they have seen practitioners in a related 'helping' profession developing, or which they have heard about second- or third-hand. Only minimal attempts have been made to adapt this to their own specialist field, even though as social workers their philosophy and primary functions have been noticeably different. In particular, they have often apparently been much impressed by the group work done in the mental health field, and have therefore regarded introspective discussion groups focused almost entirely on clients' normally unexpressed feelings, as the only 'true' way of working with groups. Here, as in other areas of their practice, they have allowed themselves to be tugged along on the coat-tails of the psychiatrist.

Alternatively, social workers have employed a 'recreational' approach, using a limited range of leisure-time activities (and especially, with adolescents, outdoor pursuits) as their medium. In this way, they have voluntarily turned themselves for the occasional weekend or week into youth leaders, or even simply into canoeing or mountaineering instructors.

The roles of psychiatrist, youth leader or outdoor activities instructor are not, of course, to be scorned or dismissed. However, their uncritical adoption by social workers has led to a great many 'one-off' stabs at 'doing group work', which have been confused in purpose and haphazard in impact. These are themes which will be examined in much greater detail elsewhere in this book. They are mentioned here merely to illustrate that group work for social workers has still far to go before it can be said to have come of age.

The casework tradition

Yet the individual social workers who have made these forays into group work cannot be held totally responsible for what has happened. Their profession as a whole has given them little encouragement to diversify their approach in any carefully thought-out and confident way. Lip-service has been paid for years to the value of group work and the need for social workers to see it as an additional medium of work. Some initial training courses now devote blocks of time to 'group dynamics', and even perhaps to 'group work theory'. In some places, substantial field resources—human or material—may also be allocated to a group work project.

Overwhelmingly, however, despite the changes which have taken place in the last decade, social work in Britain still means casework, and the assumption that it should continue to do so remains very well entrenched. Thus, on very few of the qualifying social work courses does the theoretical treatment of group work seem to be backed up by a deliberate effort regularly to provide related practical experience and supervision. Advertisements for jobs still emphasise skill in casework, while the opportunities for in-service training in group work would seem not, by any means, to meet the need.

Moreover, within their agencies, even those workers who are allowed to use or form groups may receive little credit. What they are doing is still likely to be regarded as 'experimental'—as a frill, taken on voluntarily and over and above their essential, day-to-day commitments. They will probably not get time off in lieu of the hours they have spent on their group work activities, even if these occur at weekends. And their statutory responsibilities for clients (such as those imposed on probation officers by the courts) may still have to be fulfilled through casework interviews even though the clients concerned have been met in a group.

In the light of all these pressures, it is not surprising, perhaps, that so much group work done by social workers lacks a firm theoretical basis. Nor is it surprising that the individuals who take it on, may do so without any strong personal conviction or confidence. Certainly, social workers' tentative and anxious approach to the method can be most striking (see Sturton, 1972). Repeatedly, they refer to, and worry about, 'the dark depths of group dynamics'—the powerful and dangerous forces which, they believe, groups can release. Will they, they wonder, be able to keep these in check? Or will the group run away with itself, and them? And if it does, what terrible consequences will follow?

Not all these anxieties are irrational, of course. When individuals meet in a group and form relationships which matter to them, they may indeed begin to have a powerful effect on each other, and to act collectively in forceful ways. And not all of these developments will necessarily be seen as 'good' by the social work profession. Young probationers, formed into a group, have indeed on occasion become aggressive and have made life very unpleasant for the officers involved with them. So, too, have serving prisoners within a jail, or even prospective adopters who suddenly release a flood of pent-up feelings about their failure to produce children of their own.

The social worker, then, is right to be wary of unfamiliar group situations and to demand some preparation beforehand and some support while the work is in progress. And yet not all of his fears are rational. Often they suggest a strong personal resistance to the method because of what it might do to the worker. After all, no helping method—not even one as well-tried and familiar as case-work—guarantees success. It does not even guarantee that some harm will not be done. Any encounter between human beings may end up hurting someone, temporarily or even permanently, even when one of the participants calls himself a professional social worker. And yet, because relationships can sometimes be hurtful does not mean that we do not, or should not, enter into them or try to be helpful through them.

One factor, in particular, which social workers seem not to notice about their initial reactions to group work is how closely their feelings resemble those which they almost certainly had to overcome at an earlier phase in their professional development. How did they feel as students, one wonders, as they entered their first casework interview or did their first home visit? Indeed, what were their feelings when, as a newly appointed worker, they took on full responsibility for a complete caseload? Are they in fact, when faced with the prospect of working with a group, merely shying away from the unknown—something which in previous situations they have simply not been able to do? And do they then claim that their behaviour is the result of the inadequacies or risks inherent in group work, rather than of their own uncertainties?

For the trained and experienced caseworker, such resistances are particularly out of place. For, in comparison with the beginning student or raw recruit, he has one very important advantage: he *does* have training and/or experience as a caseworker. This clearly represents a very firm base of professional expertise and personal confidence from which to venture into a 'new' method. After all, group work is not an entirely separate and distinct way of working with people. It has strong links with casework in that most of its underlying purposes, principles and values, and much of the knowledge about human personality and development, are common to both methods. The existence of this base will certainly be taken for granted throughout this book.

Nonetheless, in an atmosphere in which group work is poorly

valued and rewarded, irrational resistances and anxieties are likely to be multiplied, and are more difficult to overcome. Subtly and not-so-subtly, they are encouraged and reinforced, and legitimate reservations about the method are made to seem more powerful than in reality they are.

The North American experience

The dominance of the casework method is by no means inevitable. In countries other than Britain, and especially in North America, it has been strongly and successfully challenged. There, as in Britain, work with groups in recreational settings like youth organisations and settlements has for long been well established and well regarded. However, much more of this has been developed in a disciplined and self-conscious way than has been in Britain (Schwartz, 1966 and 1971). Also, its links with social work have been steadily strengthened until, by the 1940s, a more or less formal integration of such group work into the social work profession was achieved.

Thus today, group work in North America constitutes a recognised method of social work alongside casework and community work. Of course, such a bare statement greatly over-simplifies the true situation. Group work's acceptance by many social workers is still at best only theoretical. Those who regard themselves as caseworkers pure and simple have continued to stress the longer history of their discipline, and have assumed that it is more 'scientific', effective and prestigious. Certainly, such casework specialists have still a substantial numerical advantage. And by many of those outside professional social work circles, what they do is probably looked upon as social work's core activity.

Nonetheless, for more than three decades now, group work has been taught as a key specialism in schools of social work throughout North America. Those emerging from these courses have been employed by many field agencies because they have had this specialised training, and have been given equal opportunity with caseworkers to develop group work programmes. Indeed, some agencies have extended their methods of work as a direct response to the availability of group work specialists.

What is more, although it has taken another twenty years at least and is still not complete, a further radical development has resulted from this acceptance of group work. Social work in North America is now defining and establishing a *generic* methodology, incorporating at least the disciplines of casework and group work, and in some cases community work, too (Klein, 1970, p. 43). The aim (here) is to train social workers who can use, and feel personally comfortable in, one-to-one, group and community situations, and who can move between these as clients demand. As long as group workers in North America were struggling to gain full recognition within the social work profession—as long as they needed to prove that they could bring some quite distinctive benefits to clients—then they were probably bound to emphasise their *differences* from workers using other methods. Now that these battles have been largely won, they clearly feel that they can afford to stress their *identity* with other specialists. Indeed, it has often been the group workers who have initiated the movement for such a generic method.

And so today, instead of teaching three separate 'sequences' of casework, group work and community work, some North American schools of social work offer only a single, integrated-methods course. Practical work placements are then used which can give students broadly-based experience. As a result, more of the field agencies themselves have begun to use more than one method, and to employ workers who do not have any specialist 'method' label attached to them. Social workers in North America have thus begun to give 'genericism' an extra, and vital, dimension. And by doing so they have considerably reduced the identification of social work with casework, thereby increasing the chances that their response to clients will be flexible and appropriate.

These advances have, however, been achieved at a price—and one which, paradoxically, must be measured in terms of *reduced* flexibility and relevance. For increasingly, and quite deliberately, North American group work has in general loosened its ties—practical and theoretical—with recreational settings and has shed many of its informal educational approaches and activities. More and more it has become explicitly 'psycho-therapeutic' and 'psychiatric' in intent, and 'clinical' in manner and setting (see Vinter, 1959 and 1961). As a result, group sessions which now take place under social work's auspices seem much more often to be formally organised in agency offices, or in hospitals or other residential institutions. Many more group work meetings appear to concentrate on clarifying clients' underlying feelings and irrational attitudes, and to do this mainly through an analysis of the 'here-and-now' behaviour of individuals within the group itself.

This trend has been justified, above all, on the grounds that group workers must achieve much greater control over the helping process, and that this is possible only if they set goals which are realistically limited (Vinter, 1967a). And so, they talk less frequently of 'developing character' or 'creating good, democratic citizens', as was the wont of the old-style group workers of the settlements and youth organisations. Instead, they focus on quite narrow areas of human functioning—on clients' feelings about being illegitimate or about having produced an illegitimate child; about being childless; or about one's parents or spouse, and so on. And, as an important corollary to this, they are becoming increasingly preoccupied with 'outcomes'—with measuring as precisely as possible the impact and effectiveness of what they are doing.

The unintended, and unwanted, result of this trend, however, has in the long run been to reduce the scope of group work in North America. Values and approaches have been adopted which are familiar and acceptable to many middle class individuals, but which seem not to appeal to other social classes. In particular in the 1950s and '60s group work in North America seemed increasingly to cut itself off from those who, theoretically at least, had most need of it—the under-educated, the under-privileged and the relatively inarticulate. The US anti-poverty programmes, for this very reason, deliberately snubbed conventional social work and attempted—often very naïvely, it is true—to establish more outgoing, grass-roots-based programmes of group and community work. 'Traditional' social workers—including 'clinical' group workers —were jolted by these initiatives and some of them did modify their thinking and methods (see B. Davies, 1967). On the whole, however, their response was slow and piecemeal, and the grip of psycho-therapeutic forms of group work on American social work still remains very strong.

Future needs in Britain

All this would seem to suggest that British social work needs to consider very carefully the *forms* of group work which it wishes to encourage, before it rushes headlong into a development of group work for its own sake. In this country, psycho-analytic theory has probably never had the influence on day-to-day social work practice that it has achieved in North America. Training institutions do of course give it considerable emphasis, and so, too, does much of the literature, with the result that social workers are often made to feel that their group work should draw exclusively for its theoretical base from psycho-dynamics. Nonetheless, large numbers of British social workers in their everyday work would still seem to use such basically sociological and social psychological concepts as class, sub-culture, role and norm. Once again, they often do so in a highly intuitive way, and the impact of this 'theory' may be limited. Yet, despite the vast amount of criticism levelled at the social work profession in recent years on this score, the 'average' field practitioner seems much less likely than his North American counterpart to look upon clients as independently-functioning and internally-programmed psychological mechanisms. Rather, he is liable to respond to individuals as products, and continuing members, of significant groups and associations and of a total cultural or sub-cultural milieu.

The forms of group work which many British social workers will find most useful, therefore, will probably not be psychotherapeutically focused. These workers will on the whole be more attracted by a method which links them, and enables them to help, with the day-to-day *social* realities of their clients' lives. That is one of the reasons why this book does not assume that social workers want only to run discussion groups which are safely encapsulated in their offices and which spend most of their time contemplating their collective emotional navels. The British social worker's theoretical bias (intuitive or otherwise) must surely mean that many other kinds of group experience can be encouraged within the confines of British social work, and may prove helpful to those labelled social work clients.

What should also now be clear, however, is that this book does not assume the self-evident and indefinite superiority of casework over all other social work methods. Group work can no longer be regarded merely as light relief, or as an experimental escape, for a social worker involved in other, more central, day-to-day activities. Eileen Younghusband (1973, p. 34) has summed up the situation thus:

> Group work is used by both caseworkers and community
> workers as a necessary adjunct to or a key part of their
> work, and courses on group dynamics and participation in 'T'
> groups are common now in professional training courses.
> But this is not a substitute for the systematic study of
> small group theory and its field work application in social
> group work. It is unfortunate that we are not developing
> group work in its own right alongside the other two
> methods, when actually there is far more use than ever
> before of groups as a method in social work practice.

Thus, social work's major—sometimes even total—reliance on casework is now beginning to seem less and less logical—a leftover from the past, a historical accident which has become a contemporary anachronism. Of course, casework does, and will continue to, have a vital contribution to make. What now seems necessary, however, is a flexible and varying approach to clients, based on their highly individual and changing needs. How quickly in fact can social workers reach the point where they simply take for granted their presence in one-to-one, group and community situations and feel confident and professionally competent in dealing with any or all of these? The implications of this key question will be examined in much greater detail in the last chapter.

3

What is 'a group'?

Problems of defining 'a group'

For many social workers taking on group work roles for the first time, one somewhat academic question frequently seems to overshadow all others: What do we mean by 'a group', anyway? Here, it often seems, is a major theoretical obstacle which has to be cleared away before any practical progress can be made.

It is doubtful, however, if the question 'What is a group?' can ever be finally answered. Despite long and abstruse discussions, argument seems invariably to persist. Take the matter of the *size* of a group, for example. It may be readily agreed that most social workers are concerned with small groups. But, do *two* people constitute such a group? Or must there be at least *three*? And when does a small group cease to be small and become large, or even a crowd? When its numbers have risen to ten? To twenty? Or higher?

And what about the *physical properties* of a group? Must all individuals be in the same place at the same time for the group to be said to be in existence? Or does the group continue to exist even when its members are geographically dispersed, even if only by a few yards or miles?

Then there are questions about *time*: How long have individuals to be in contact with each other before it can be said that they constitute a group? Must they meet at least fortnightly for a minimum of two hours? What if they meet for just ten minutes each week or on six occasions only in the year? Can they then be said to be a group?

Finally, there are questions of *perspective*: who says that a gathering of individuals is, or is not, a group? Does the group really exist if only outsiders call the gathering a group, without the individuals to whom they are referring, feeling or knowing of their collective identity? Or must this subjective sense of belonging exist too?

None of these, of course, is a totally irrelevant question. They raise or imply issues which, for very practical purposes, do need to be considered and if possible clarified. Anyone trying to work with groups in a disciplined way needs to understand how and why an individual comes to sense his own involvement with other individuals, and how and why he is willing to commit himself to them.

Unfortunately, however, many discussions on 'What is a group?' seem not to have this practical purpose. Instead, they seem to be carried on as if, by verbal exchange, the participants will be able to discover some carefully concealed definition of 'group' which is divinely inspired, and therefore final, perfect and worthy of blind emulation in their practice. It is a form of Utopian thinking which in the long run is unlikely to be helpful to the practitioner.

Such an ultimate definition of 'group' can probably never be achieved because, *in reality*, groups do not exist as discrete, concrete entities. They are not, perhaps figments of our imagination. But they are, formulations of the human mind. That is, the word 'group' is no more than a way of summarising and expressing a very wide and complicated range of human experiences and phenomena. True, in recent years, some elements of this summary have gained quite widespread acceptance, and the probability of their occurring has been tested by experiment. Nonetheless, the term 'group' provides no more than an approximate and subjective representation of the 'realities' of human experience, and this representation is in many respects quite arbitrary.

Moreover, as has already been made clear (see Chapter 1), 'set-piece' situations are not the only ones in which a group work perspective might be helpful. A great variety of (to an onlooker) ill-defined, only partially formed, and very fluid situations might also call for the application of group work insights because, in them, the *interaction* between individuals is crucial. Family 'interviews', encounters with three or more clients in the waiting-room or the street, at school or at their place of work, 'social clubs', tenants groups and other neighbourhood groups, 'recreational activity groups'—all these and many others potentially constitute such situations. In them, it may be vital that a worker understand and utilise the exchanges between people, rather than just develop and exploit his own direct relationship with each of them individually. This therefore makes it even more difficult to produce a single and final definition of 'group'.

A working definition of 'group'

In the statements that follow, therefore, a selection has been made of those elements of collective human behaviour and experience which seem to me to fit the needs and purposes of those who are most likely to read this book. It is thus a 'definition' of 'group' which is by no means definitive. Rather, it bears in mind where, how and under what circumstances, this plurality of individuals might meet and operate. And so, when in this book reference is made to a group, it is intended to imply:

> A gathering of three or more individual human beings;
> who may, but who may not, expect to go on meeting
> permanently; in which direct person-to-person exchanges
> (verbal or non-verbal) between *each* individual are at least
> possible; and in which there exists, *or is possible*,
> between and among these individuals some common
> interests and/or purposes, some sense of identity and some
> mutual acceptance of interdependence.

The base-line of this definition—'three or more individual human beings'—is intended to highlight (firstly) that, even though we are discussing group situations, it is still uniquely *individual* personalities which are involved (and secondly it is meant to emphasise), that being involved with a third person (and also of course a fourth, fifth, sixth and so on) modifies, not only this individuality, but also the *exchanges* between just two individuals. Thus, in the diagram

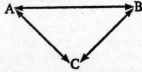

the intervention of C not only affects A as a person and B as a person; it also alters the interaction between A and B. A and B are thus likely to respond to each other, as well as to other elements in their situation (including, of course, other individuals such as D, E and so on), to some degree differently from the way they would have responded if C were not present. It is this possibility of modifying the relationship between individuals because of the intervention of other individuals which is crucial to our conception of a group.

This definition, though quite categorically laying down a minimum size for a group, is much less specific about an upper limit, and indeed deliberately avoids stating this in numerical terms.

It does assume the *possibility* of direct person-to-person exchanges among *all* the individuals. And this, even though it may never become a reality, inevitably sets a 'natural' limit on the size of the group. The *actual* maximum number among whom such direct communication and contact could be achieved may vary somewhat according to circumstances. In some cases it may be as few as three, in others rather more. It is, however, an unmistakable way of distinguishing this type of small group from say, a crowd or a mob.

This insistence on the possibility, at least, of direct, person-to-person interaction among all participants has another practical consequence. It means that on some occasions anyway, and for some periods of time, all participants must be gathered in physical proximity. Again, it is not necessary to be specific; indeed, it is not possible to be specific, since once again the circumstances of the group will vary. Nonetheless, this criterion of at least potential face-to-face exchange does in a general way deal with the spatial and time elements of group life, as well as with group size.

The problems of time, space and size are also dealt with indirectly in the suggestion that common purposes and/or interests, and a sense of identity and interdependence, should (actually or potentially) exist among individuals involved in the collective situation. This is even more of an evaluative criterion than those suggested so far, even more dependent on the subjective interpretations of a supposedly objective onlooker. And again, in practice, such identity and interdependence may never establish themselves—they may remain forever potential. Nonetheless, even given a change in one or more of the variables in this situation—the physical environment, what the individuals are doing and so on—the fact that it *could* exist, has important implications. Again it suggests that time may be needed, and that for some of this time individuals need to be a physical proximity.

Nonetheless, though there are indications of what may be involved, the definition is deliberately vague about maximum size, where the gathering meets and especially how much time is needed. By being imprecise in this way, allowance is thus once again made for these situations of collective human exchange which are spontaneous and transient, but which, in social work terms anyway, may be at least potentially productive. Take, for example, those passing and accidental combinations of individuals which are formed or emerge to deal with a crisis (like a sudden bereavement in a neighbourhood). They may never subsequently reform in exactly the same way. However, while they last, they produce a very strong feeling among participants of being involved with each other, and might be particularly beneficial to some individuals if they are deliberately supported and encouraged.

Or, take those informal, often social and recreational events like a youngsters' street 'kick-about' or a small gathering of mere acquaintances in a pub. Here again, the combination of individuals is likely, in its original form, to be impermanent and ostensibly superficial in its impact. But again, the individuals might already feel some investment with each other, or might begin to do so given some new opportunity or reason. The interactions which exist could thus be extremely helpful to them, even though no formal 'group' has ever been recognised or defined.

For social workers, these unplanned group situations could offer new, perhaps once-for-all, perhaps more long-term, openings for providing appropriate help. No definition of group should, in itself, discourage them from applying any group work insights and skills they possess to such situations. The need for a constantly active, interactionist perspective must again be stressed.

The insistence in the definition on an actual or potential sense of identity and interdependence has another useful consequence. It by-passes those incessant theoretical and largely sterile discussions about all those situations in which a number of individuals— passengers in a railway compartment, patients in a doctor's waiting-room and so on—happen to be in the same place at the same time, without having any direct need for or concern with *each other*. The question that seems permanently to fascinate is: Do they or do they not constitute a group?

It is of course true that an accident—the sudden illness of one of the passengers, the doctor's non-arrival for surgery—may create some, even temporary, feeling of identity among these separate individuals. By our definition, they might then be a group which, hypothetically anyway, could 'use' or 'be used' by, a social worker. And the steps by which they move from a state of separation from each other, to greater mutual involvement might theoretically be exploitable. (At the very least, all this might help to illustrate some of the very early difficulties, described more fully in Chapter 5, which may be encountered when people who were previously strangers to each other first congregate.)

For most practical purposes, however, the question 'Are such gatherings *really* groups?' seems largely irrelevant to most social workers. What, above all, the social worker needs to know is: Are such gatherings usable: can they, in their present form, help him to fulfil his purposes, or at least, are they, in any realistic sense, capable of development so that they can be so helpful? Unless the answers to these questions are clearly positive, the whole debate must remain almost entirely academic.

Indeed, the main purpose of discussing what is meant by the term 'group' has throughout been very practical—hence, in part, the vagueness and flexibility of the definition offered. Social workers should feel confident about moving within a very wide variety of situations of human interaction as they arise. And they should feel able to use them in ways best suited to their clients' needs. They should be able to form groups deliberately for a period of time to be determined by them and/or by the clients involved. They should be able to intervene in groups which already exist (assuming of course that they do this in ethical ways which are acceptable to the group members). They should be able to recognise and utilise short-term and spontaneous interactional situations which lack any formal definition. And ideally they should be able to combine any or all these approaches as and when appropriate, both with each other, and also with a casework approach. If they are really to adjust their ideas of time, space, size and content according to the nature of the interactions and the people involved, then an absolute, handed-down definition of groups will be of very little use to them.

The definition in practice

Much of what has been offered so far has, however, amounted to little more than a negative definition of a group. A much more positive conceptualisation of the term is clearly needed if practitioners are to feel that their understanding and actions are being in any way guided.

A number of ways of achieving such a conceptualisation are, of course, available. Three such formulations are presented below and their relative usefulness for the social worker examined. Though selected in a rather arbitrary way, they do seem to represent views, held by many social workers, on what it is they are working with when they enter group situations.

1. *A group as a centre for practical activity* Very often those who work with a group see it primarily as a place in which quite practical tasks are tackled. In describing what they themselves do, therefore, social workers will talk of: 'sharing with colleagues the instruction in rock-climbing and canoeing'; 'being available to complete a foursome for a card-game'; or 'arranging transport and materials for the children'. No comment—explicit or implicit—seems to be needed on the individuals who comprise these situations and work on these tasks, or on their interaction with each

25

other. The *raison d'être* of a group is apparently what it *does*.

2. *A group as a gathering of a number of individuals who meet together in the same place at the same time to work on the same or similar tasks*   A second, common view of a group is rather less simplistic. This recognises some, at least, of its human processes while suggesting that, on the whole, the individuals involved mainly operate independently of each other. Workers who hold this conception of a group thus say about their own functions:

'I get an opportunity to give individual advice in a relaxed and informal atmosphere.'
'I usually find myself talking with one of the five boys in particular.'
'The number of workers in the group has recently increased to allow individuals to receive even more attention.'

If the focus *is* on the client's rather than the worker's contribution to the group and its life, it often highlights the individual elements of the situation:

'One boy is extremely noisy, attention-seeking and hostile.'
'One man seems very dependent on me for advice and information.'
'The girls are all incapable of sustaining interest in anything the group does for more than a short time.'

Such a view of a group seems above all to imply that a number of individuals happen to be together in the same place at the same time. They may even be working jointly on the same task, or in parallel or similar tasks. However, in the eyes of the worker, it seems, they continue by and large to function as independent personalities, each of whose dynamic comes from within. No one individual apparently has any significant formative influence on the unique personality or behaviour of any other individual. And, as far as the worker is concerned, no *collective* human experience is generated which is different in kind from what each individual might have encountered if he had pursued the same task on his own.

Many social workers might well reject such a view of 'a group'. They might believe that they assume or even emphasise the interrelatedness and interdependence of individuals. Nonetheless, in their almost casual descriptions of what they are doing in groups, social workers do seem frequently to imply a conceptualisation of 'a group' which virtually ignores this interactionist viewpoint. Training, and much else in their previous experience, may have en-

trenched one-person-at-a-time perceptions which continue to dominate how they think about their group work practice and even
what they actually do within it. And yet as Klein (1970, p. 53) has
pointed out, 'the worker who focuses on an individual in the
group is not utilizing group process and, hence is neglecting the
very essence of the growth or therapeutic quality inherent in the
group'.

*3. A group as a developing organism composed of interacting and
interdependent individuals* Defining an alternative to one-person-
at-a-time perceptions can lead to the accusation—and accusation it
usually is—that the group is being made an end in itself which must
be developed and preserved because, *as a collectivity*, it is valuable.
This is an issue which is examined in detail in Chapter 4.

When attempting to conceptualise a group, however, a social
worker might start with the proposition that individuals may
jointly generate experiences which are felt as special by each
individual because of their interactional content, without making
the group an end in its own right. Thus, the uniqueness of this situation does not exist solely in the individuality of the personalities
taking part. It exists also in their interrelatedness, which contributes
to, and helps to define and even to create, that individuality.

For a social worker, therefore, the focus of concern may need
to be this *reciprocation*, and this individually *creative inter-*
dependence. On occasions, it may operate in quite practical areas,
such as in the initiation or development of key tasks:

'One man has a "flair" for making toys. Now a number of other
men who know him are also busily occupied with toy making.'
'A leader emerged very quickly to give the group project an
enormous push.'

On other occasions, the impact may be much more on standards
and values:

'The habit of poking fun at Joe, who stammers, fell away after he
brought the materials for the group. Quite soon after this, a
brief discussion developed on what it feels like to be victimised
for something you can't help.'

Or the emergent interdependence may influence feelings:

'Newcomers' sensitivity at being physically handicapped seemed
to lessen after they had attended several meetings. They certainly made fewer references to their handicaps and didn't
apologise as often.'

27

'Some members were aggressive and difficult to fit in at first, and they were often treated very roughly. Now the group seems much more accepting of this sort of behaviour.'

Put together in this way, quotations of this sort from social workers' own accounts of practice can read very much like a series of success stories. They are not offered, however, as *evaluations* of what happens in groups. Rather, they are intended as *descriptions*. They are meant to suggest what can happen when individuals come together, act together, react to each other and become reciprocally involved. The outcomes may be 'good' or 'bad' depending on the value system employed. But the individuals concerned may end up thinking, believing and feeling very differently from how they might have thought, believed and felt if they had remained unconnected with, and uncommitted to, each other.

According to this view, therefore, a group needs to be conceived as an organism—what the *Oxford Dictionary* defines as 'an organised body with connected interdependent parts sharing a common life'. Such a body is not, of course, static and unchanging. The parts within it are continually readjusting to each other, realigning themselves, reorganising the tactics as well as, on occasions, the strategy of their interdependence.

Thus, not only does a group change; it might even *develop*, in the sense of evolving a more complex organisation of its internal inter-connections than that from which it started. And it might also by certain stated criteria, *progress*—from a lesser to a greater effective-ness, from a lesser to a greater capacity collectively to perform the tasks on which it is engaged. In either of these senses, therefore, a group may be regarded as an evolving organism.

Such evolution is never, of course, inevitable. A collection of individuals may meet the basic conditions laid down in the definition of group offered earlier—three or more individuals with the possibility of direct communication among them, and of evolv-ing common interests, a sense of identity and of mutual inter-dependence. And yet these possibilities may never be realised, so that development and progress (as against simple change) never actually take place. An organism can remain very simple in its organisation, and may never improve on its initial effectiveness to do its work, and yet may still be an organism.

Nonetheless, this third way of conceptualising a group can be of crucial importance to the social worker. For it suggests that he work, not only with the individuals as individuals, but also with

the way they organise their interconnections and interrelatedness
(Klein, 1970, pp. 52-4).

Thus, when the social worker sees person A, he certainly needs
to take into account that person's distinctive characteristics, talents,
modes of self-expression and so on. But he must also in effect, ask:
In what ways, and at what points, are what I see as 'distinctively
person A' the product (at least in part) of his or her connectedness
to persons B, C, D, etc (as well as, incidentally, to me, the social
worker)? For, what the social worker in a group shares is a
collective experience of himself with A, B, C, D, etc. in which, in
part, each individual self-presentation is special to that particular,
here-and-now situation of human exchange. He may not, of course,
ever be able to grasp every detail and constituent element of that
situation. But, as a group worker, he needs to be allowing continually for its repercussions, and to be working with, and on, them
quite specifically.

In fact, for the group worker, a group has to be seen as 'both the
means and the context of treatment' (Vinter, 1967c). In other words,
a group is not just *a place, an arena*, in which help is provided for
one individual, for another individual, and another, and another,
whether simultaneously or one at a time. Rather, a group is *a
vehicle* which collectively moves the individuals concerned—often
in important ways, and also, perhaps, in spite of the worker's
attempt to steer it. A social worker, to be a group worker, therefore
needs to conceptualise group so that he emphasises both the
vehicle's internal combustion and also his own need to use *this*
in the best interests of all those caught up in its movement.

4
Why use groups?

It has been suggested a number of times already that, when individuals interact in a group, they set in motion some distinctive and influential processes. The question needs to be asked, however: How, even potentially, are these processes beneficial? What ends, regarded as desirable in social work, might in fact be served by them?

Group work and social work's strategic purposes

The key underlying response of this book to such questions can be stated baldly: purposes and ethics which are accepted as proper for casework will normally continue to apply when the social worker begins to act as a group worker. In other words, what the social worker regards as desirable and legitimate does not automatically alter merely because he has changed his mode of operation. The desirable and the legitimate are determined by beliefs, values and knowledge which apply to social work and the social work profession as such, and not just to the particular method being adopted.

Thus, the caseworker may define his overall—strategic—objectives as 'enhancing social functioning', as 'building ego strengths' and/or as 'helping clients to achieve radical changes in their society'. Because he then moves into the group work situation, these purposes will not suddenly become irrelevant or obsolete.

Moreover, the carryover will occur even if he states his objectives in less universal and more individual terms—if he talks rather of 'trying to stop Johnny getting into trouble again', or of 'helping Mrs Smith cope with her family while her husband is "away"', or of 'helping Mr and Mrs Jones to get better housing'. And—as these examples should make clear—the carryover of purpose will exist regardless of whether the social worker chooses to emphasise the social-control or social-change elements in his purpose.

The underlying assumption here, of course, is that no particular purposes or ethics are attached or integral to any particular method. Rather, it is assumed that the same method may be used, perhaps by different individuals or bodies, to seek very different ends. Some of these aims may even be directly contradictory to, or even sharply in conflict with, each other.

And so, some work with groups will undoubtedly be regarded by social workers as irrelevant or even valueless—perhaps much of what is done with groups by industry would fall into such a category. Some of it might even be seen by social workers as positively evil, like, no doubt, most of what Hitler or Stalin did to manipulate group (including family group) relationships. However, the purpose and content of work in groups may be so formulated that it more than adequately fulfils the values and ethics already accepted by social workers. The consequent group work can then be regarded as social work conducted in, and through, group encounters, and so can be called 'social group work'.

Thus social work with groups has to be seen as a tactical manoeuvre intended to help a worker get closer to goals, within a pattern of ethics, which are independently defined. Simply because he has for some of his time gone over to group work does not mean that he must suddenly cast around frantically for new justifications and guidelines for his work and his role in society.

Individualising the group member

All this may seem an unnecessarily long restatement of the obvious. And yet, the confusion between means and ends can occur very easily when social workers adopt what they see as a 'new' way of working. They may too readily conclude that, because they are modifying their methods, then their purposes and ethics, too, must be adjusted.

One issue over which such confusion seems most likely to occur is that of individualising the client and his needs. After all, by definition, group work focuses on 'the group', and may emphasise the importance and influence of the collectivity to the point where 'group-centredness' seems paramount. In the process, 'the individual' may appear to lose all significance, or at least to be no longer the social worker's central concern.

Such a conclusion, however, greatly distorts what group work can and, in a social work context, normally would be about. For, in the first place, it again overlooks the fact that the group is

intended primarily to be a *medium* through which help is offered—
one means of attaining independently-stated or acknowledged goals.

It is true, of course, that the cohesion of the group may need to
be strong. If, in other words, group members do not feel a real pull
towards the group, an identity with other group members and a
willingness to act collectively to achieve common ends, then the
value to them of their group experience may be very limited. This
does not mean, however, that the group has become an end in itself.
The group's existence is not thereby justified, or its value proved,
merely because these shared feelings exist within the group. For the
social worker, the validation of the group's activities can normally
only come when individuals, as individuals, say or feel that they
have taken something *for themselves* from being a group member,
or when an 'objective' observer can recognise such individual gains.
The pay-off is made to people, and not to some impersonal, abstract
entity we choose to term 'the group'.

In practice, the picture is inevitably more complex than such
bald statements make it appear. After all, the 'something' which
individuals take for themselves may, paradoxically, be a new or
strengthened feeling of having given something to others. Or it may
be an awareness of having been allowed by others to co-exist with
them—of having belonged. It may even be that for the first time
they have *allowed* themselves to belong, since fellow-feeling,
mutuality and an out-going conscience—often called 'a sense of
community'—can be as valuable as 'individuality' and 'autonomy'.
This may also mean that the 'something' which they have gained is
in fact their *submission* to the demands and pressures of group
membership. For conformity can be most acceptable to an individual, and even pleasurable and beneficial. And this may be particularly true if, as with many social work clients, they have regularly
in the past known only rejection and isolation.

In addition, it has to be acknowledged that, in practice, not all
social work anyway is about helping individuals to be more independent. Social workers may, of course, protest loudly—perhaps
too loudly—about this. But, the social control elements of their
function are important, and often in reality paramount. They are
inevitably at times, called in where individuals *have* to be helped to
adjust to their social circumstances—to, say, an inescapable network of face-to-face family relationships, or to society's legal, or
other, constraints. An experience of conforming to a 'successful'
or 'beneficial' group may then be extremely helpful: it may teach
them how such enforced adjustment to circumstances can be a
little more satisfactorily accomplished.

These qualifications, however, do not fundamentally alter the central argument. For most social workers in most group work situations the group needs not, in any practical sense, be an end in itself. They usually have little reason to measure ultimate 'success' by the strength of the collective feelings, goals and attitudes which they help to establish. As in so many other of his operations, the social worker's key evaluation will be of individuals, of how their self-image, feelings about themselves, and ability to act autonomously have gained.

Some general advantages of group work

Insisting that group work is an integral part of social work and is therefore concerned with the same central purposes as all social work activity is not, however, to suggest that working in groups offers no special, at least potential, advantages. It is true that such advantages usually have to be stated in very generalised terms and so can be difficult to operationalise. They must focus mainly on what, overall and in the long-term, social workers hope will emerge from their activities, and must tend therefore to be universalist in scope and ideal, even Utopian, in conception.

Nonetheless, for social workers approaching group work for the first time, and probably rather tentatively, such a clarification of general objectives can provide some practical guidelines and a useful impetus.

1. The normality of group experience Firstly, it is perhaps necessary to state explicitly that group work experience is so familiar to every individual that it would be sheer perversity not to use it more often. Indeed it might be argued that, for most people, it is the experience of being in a group which is normal, and the one-to-one private confrontation which is strange.

Certainly, in our society, individuals cannot avoid regular and personally-involving entanglements in group situations. First in the family, then at school, work and leisure, and ultimately (for most people) in a new family when they marry and have children, they are continuously exposed to group experience.

Indeed, for our own *individual* benefit, this intimate involvement with others is not only inevitable—it is essential. For it does more than ensure that we have the material and emotional necessities of human life—food, clothing, security, love and so on. It also gives us the feedback about our own personality and our impact on others, which is vital if we are to establish and confirm our independent existence. It is, of course, often argued that the opposite is true: that group membership, and the pressures which this brings, undermine the uniqueness and autonomy of the individual. And on some occasions, and to some extent, this must undoubtedly happen. But it is at least equally true that, without group experience, individual personality would not just be less well developed—it would simply not exist. 'Significant others' provide models against which emergent personalities can and do test their uniqueness. Even more important, they (and less significant individuals we encounter also) act as mirrors, reflecting who and what we are, or are becoming. As we shall see in more detail later (see pp. 57-9), if we did not have group experience through which to experiment, confirm ourselves, and gain some measure of how others perceive us, we would not have a 'self' at all.

Group experience is thus both normal and vital for each individual. Is the same true of the one-to-one situation? Clearly, every individual very early in life depends heavily on the intensive one-to-one involvement of child-mother, and also child-father, relationships, which have very long-lasting effects. And throughout life, they will probably meet, and welcome, private moments with just one other person; indeed, these can provide, like the small group situation, many important opportunities for discovering and establishing the individual self. In that sense, therefore, in so far as they *do* occur, one-to-one encounters are no less valuable for personal development.

But, how often *do* they occur? How normal are they? How familiar and at ease are most people in such meetings? On the whole, they are less frequent than group experience. Even that most common and influential of one-to-one relationships—marriage— does not, for most people, remain unaffected by the intrusion of other individuals (especially children) for very long. And few other 'dyads' have the status or impact of that of husband and wife. It is hardly surprising, therefore, that in our society individuals are less familiar with one-to-one than with group encounters, and that they feel less comfortable within them.

Moreover, this lack of familiarity and comfort may well be particularly noticeable amongst those individuals whom social workers meet most often, since, within the social class from which most social work clients are drawn, opportunities for private one-to-one meetings are probably limited. Certainly, within working class sectors of our society, families have for long been thrown closely together in small and overcrowded houses. Peer group associations —among adolescents, housewives, workmates, pub mates and so on—still play an important part in their lives. Where neighbourhood activity has been, or remains, high, a further source of regular, intimate group experience exists.

Inevitably, therefore, the moments when just two individuals come together for any length of time for a serious purpose are quite rare. Moreover, most such occasions in social work rely heavily on verbalisation, and therefore may be even less welcome to working class clients, for whom the type and specialised use of words normal to a casework interview seem to have lower priority than non-verbal exchanges. Such individuals might meet in pairs to play cribbage, or shop or child-mind or drink tea. And, while doing so, they might converse quite freely, and with considerable, appropriate articulateness for the occasion. Merely to sit down in a ritualised way to talk at length in a rather formalised language about personal matters with just one other person, would normally be seen as strange.

None of this is intended to suggest that individuals, whatever their class background, do not some time need to discuss matters privately with one other person, or that they will inevitably be incapable of doing so. Indeed, it could be argued that, *because* we spend so much of our time in groups perhaps suppressing or disguising our own special needs, we need all the opportunities we can get to be the sole focus of someone else's interest. Rather, the intention has been to emphasise how normal group experience is for everyone and how helpful it might therefore be if it were used more often and more deliberately by social workers, at least with some of their clients.

2. *Changing perceptions and self-perceptions* This, however, justifies group work only in the most general terms. The question still remains: By working deliberately with groups, what might the social worker achieve that he is not already achieving?

For social worker and clients who normally meet privately, experience in a group can provide valuable new perceptions of individuals and their situation. In part, perceptions may alter merely because the circumstances of meeting have changed. In addition, however, some of the factors intrinsic to group experience are so relevant to what social worker and client are trying to achieve that involvement in a group can be particularly revealing.

For, in a group, each individual is required to negotiate situations —to perform tasks, take on roles, fulfil expectations and standards, share in feelings and so on—which may, in themselves, be like those which the client finds difficult in other, key areas of his life. On occasions, of course, this may be true, too, of the one-to-one interview. However, in such a setting, it seems more likely that these situations of difficulty for the client will be dealt with only indirectly, symbolically, mainly through verbal description and analysis.

Social work experience in a group, however, is more likely to *reproduce* what a client actually does and feels in certain key relationships. It may become a microcosm of much more personally significant forms of the client's social intercourse—a forum in which the client meets and has to deal with those very types of social encounter which he finds painful and in which his embarrassment, incomprehension, lack of competence, unrecognised strengths and so on are revealed.

In other words, social work with groups seems much more likely to *demonstrate first-hand* what is inhibiting a client's social development and damaging his current relationships with others. As a result, a worker may actually be able to *share* some of the experiences with which a client is struggling rather than just hearing about them, and so, too, may others (such as fellow-clients). It may then become possible for the client himself to look again at his problems, in a different, and hopefully more supportive, atmosphere :

> The improvisation this afternoon revolved round gang-fighting. The girls were assumed, without question, to play extremely dependent roles, and in particular to show admiration and approval for the boys' masculine prowess. In this sense their physical handicaps were irrelevant, since such a situation might have arisen in any adolescent group. However, Ray's behaviour was particularly striking, since, as far as his two sticks would allow him, he raced around acting extremely aggressively and making very direct and often intimidating bids for the girls' attention. He strove throughout to behave as if his handicap did not exist, and as if he was of course the answer to every girl's dream. At one point, I overheard Debbie say, to no-one in particular : 'He's stupid.' If he heard her, he certainly took no notice (Physically Handicapped Adolescent Group).

This clarity of perception is not of course a one-way process. It is possible, too, that in a group, the worker and what he is trying to do may come to be seen more clearly. After all, the client may, as was suggested earlier, be more familiar with group situations. He may therefore feel more at ease and so marginally more open to the worker as a person and to what the worker is communicating, verbally and non-verbally. And the worker in turn may be able to depend less on describing to the client how others can act helpfully towards him; he may himself be able to demonstrate more directly what this can mean, or help others to do the same.

Thus, clients may come to feel less threatened by the worker. For, a social work group will often contain others very like the client, who are also cast in the client role. And these others may be seen at the very least as potential supporters against any felt or actual threat from the worker. Certainly, more than one social worker has reported how clients who have always seemed ill-at-ease, resentful and defensive in social work situations, have very rapidly—almost too rapidly—thawed out when met in a group, or in their 'natural' group surroundings.

The group (of teenage girls) began to talk about parents and how they treated teenage children, especially girls. I think it was Jenny who introduced the topic, but it was taken up enthusiastically by Ellen and by Fran.... Quite suddenly, Maggie, who had remained silent throughout the discussion, as she had very largely in the two previous meetings, launched into a bitter and deeply felt attack on her father. She described how he beat her if she was home even two minutes late at night, how he locked her clothes up to prevent her going out, how he broke her records, and much else. She even implied he took some sexual liberties when he used physical force on her.... Maggie has normally talked quite easily with me in the past, when I've seen her in the office, and has often discussed apparently real and personal concerns such as boy-friends. But she has never even as much as indicated that the relationship with her father is so bad, even though I've suspected the problem and tried to encourage her to talk about it. Tonight, she was like a dam burst (Community Home Girls' Group).

By the time I arrived at the club this afternoon, the women had been gathered for about twenty minutes.... Mrs Jones (who only started coming last week, when I was away) was at the centre of a chattering little group of three or four and had them hanging on to her every word. She seemed totally unaware of her children even when one of them got into a fight. Mrs Graham, who'd been one of this little group, later told me it had been the best meeting for ages, and asked whether the bus ran direct to Heskin St (where Mrs Jones lives). Whenever I've seen Mrs Jones at home, she has invariably been morose and withdrawn. She seemed to be snapping at the kids incessantly (almost for my benefit!) and was always too busy to sit down and talk (Wives' Club).

This increase in motivation at least to become engaged with a social work service is of course extremely important. But a change in the client's self-perception and in his perception of others (including social workers) can have real and sometimes even immediate and practical effects. It can in fact be therapeutic in its own right. Seeing and feeling oneself differently, and seeing and feeling significant others (especially authority figures) differently, can in itself do much to alter attitudes, behaviour and relationships in important ways.

Although the emphasis here is clearly on the new information and insights which the interactional situation can produce—on what in social work is traditionally called 'diagnosis'—this term has quite deliberately been avoided. For, what it seems usually to imply is that the worker's role is a static one, and that *his* behaviour and *his* image in the eyes of the client, as well as his *self* image, remain unchanged throughout his interaction with the client. Indeed, social work diagnosis frequently seems to mean that information and interpretations are collected and presented only *for the client*. During this operation, apparently, *the worker* has no impact on, or meaning for, the client, or, if he does, these are of no significance.

Whatever may be true for casework, such a conception of diagnosis certainly cannot hold for group work. The knowledge and perceptions which are being gathered or altered by experience in a group are likely to concern and affect *all* the participants, *including* the worker. Interaction is not selective. It can never leave out one participating individual, however great his power or elevated his status.

3. *A reduced sense of isolation* Another way in which group experience can bring about change in a client's behaviour and situation is by reducing a client's sense of isolation. By definition, a group brings a client into some form of contact with other individuals. This in itself may not, of course, help him feel less alone. Indeed, if these others are very different from him (say in social competence) or indifferent to him, he can end up feeling even more isolated. This would be merely the extra loneliness which comes from being alone in a crowd.

However, a group has *the potential* to produce a very different outcome, especially if group members do have some interests and circumstances in common and if, perhaps with help, they can become more conscious of these common areas. Indeed, given such a development, a client's gain need not only be the negative one: 'I am not alone.' It can also be very positive, in that the client is also saying, 'I and these others are alike', or even 'We belong together'. Moreover, in some circumstances, the gains can be very practical—regular and reliable baby-sitters, an exchange of children's clothes, well-liked drinking companions or playmates—so that the reduction of isolation can be felt very real.

What this also re-emphasises is that the sources of potential help for clients are automatically increased when he enters a group. Again, the help *is* only potential. But, given some favourable circumstances and a well-judged social work contribution, then every group member can be regarded as a possible resource for every other group member. What is more, this help might be as valuable and as effective as any offered by the worker, if not more so. Within a group, clients may at different times need acceptance, reassurance and support, or practical advice, or material assistance. Or, they may need control or some direct confrontation with their own characteristics and impact on others. The person best able to provide any of these is at least as likely to be another client as the worker. What is more, because such help is being offered by a *peer* rather than by some remote, suspect or at least vaguely 'foreign' authority figure, it may also be accepted much more readily.

> Jamie's early attendance at the Centre was erratic, and when he did come (even if it was still morning) he was usually drunk or suffering a hang-over. The other men—though many were heavy drinkers themselves—poked (often unkind) fun at him, or showed open irritation and hostility. And the (probation) officer's efforts of persuasion or reprimand made absolutely no difference. The one exception to all this was Bill, who from the start took a liking to Jamie, befriended him in a way no PO ever had or could, and influenced the attitude of everybody at the Centre to Jamie. After a couple of months, Jamie's drinking bouts were much less frequent, or anyway seemed not to be having the old effects of missed days at work, fighting and social isolation (Day Treatment Centre).

4. *Rehearsing new ways of behaving* The corollary of this, of course, is that controlled experience in a group can also provide clients with very real opportunities for giving as well as for receiving help. For many individuals who find themselves in the role of client, this may be an unfamiliar experience, since for them dependence on, or subjection to, authority is probably the norm. Only exceptionally do they feel themselves to be people with resources and traits which are needed and valued by others. And, as was suggested in Chapter 1, the very term 'client' may encourage feelings of inferiority, and may force the individual so labelled, into the position of mere recipient.

Involvement in a group makes a break out of this straitjacket possible, for both worker and clients. Roles can be reversed, so to speak. Clients can gain experience of themselves being helpful— being sympathetic and supportive, or frank, or the donor of essential information or even of material services. They can also gain experience of themselves doing what the worker—the expert, the authority—cannot do, or cannot do as well.

> By this time, Fran was in tears, and talking almost uncontrollably. She could not imagine how she was ever going to pick up the pieces of her life again. Ellen, without saying a word, put her arm round her so that Fran was able to collapse slowly against her until her head was on Ellen's shoulder. And Maggie said, very quietly: 'Yes, it really is a sod, isn't it?' I wasn't sure how to react, but I did say as quietly as I could: 'Yes, I'm sure Ellen understands that.' (Community Home Girls' Group).

> At the end of the improvisation, as we sat around breathless and excited, comments began to come about what we'd done and how well it had gone. Becky was by now at her most hyperactive, while Eric was actually managing to raise his head and look at the others as they spoke. I asked why they were so pleased, and then, later, who had done most to make it go so well. Jenny then said she thought Ray had been very cruel to Eric and had really shown him up. 'Who were you trying to kid?' she added. Ray coloured and again tried to change the topic, but Maggie chipped in, too. A fascinating discussion then began about Ray's way of 'carrying on' in the group, how he used Eric to make himself seem big, and how this made the girls feel uncomfortable. For most of the time, Ray said nothing; he just looked sulky and withdrawn (Physically Handicapped Adolescent Group).

Playing the 'helper' role for a change, rather than always being the person helped is, however, only one specific example of how such controlled group experience can enable clients to behave in, for them, untried or neglected ways. A later chapter will discuss in much greater detail the variety of behavioural demands which a group makes of its members—how it asks or impels them to play roles, adhere to standards, perform tasks, express feelings and so on. These of course may merely repeat, and so reinforce, forms of behaviour already being revealed outside the group. But again, with some well-judged help, they may break or reduce such habits so that here, too, they may give the client a new sense of himself and of what is right and possible for him.

Such experimentation with self is likely to occur in a group only if individuals feel secure and accepted within that group. This, of course, is only another way of saying that, paradoxically, what is experimental for the individual may in practice be extremely conformist in the context of any particular group. That is, the individual may do things in a group which are new for him only because they enable him to adhere to what other group members expect and allow. Such conformity is of course often condemned for undermining individuality and personal freedom. In fact, however, it is possible to see it as a further illustration of how 'the self' is defined and extended, rather than diminished, through exacting exchanges with others.

In any case, this view of individuals totally subservient to the demands of a group is greatly oversimplified. Much individual be-haviour in a group may be of this conformist kind. But not all. As (again perhaps with skilled help) a group develops cohesion and confidence, then acceptable non-conformity may become possible, and may even sometimes be encouraged. What one writer has called a 'deviational allowance' (see Shulman, 1971) begins to operate, which permits individuals to rehearse new and (by group standards) unconventional types of behaviour, without necessarily being rejected or ridiculed.

Whether conforming to group standards or not, the importance of this particular aspect of group experience for an *individual's* needs should not be underestimated. Being a member of a group can allow an individual to rehearse new ways of behaving. And this can often be an enormous gain for clients who too often have been forced by present circumstances and past experience into rigid moulds of activity, and, above all, into stereotyped and restricted self-images.

I noticed at the next club meeting that Mrs Williams, who always looked so worn out and unkempt when I saw her at home or in the street, was wearing a bright pinafore dress and blouse which I'd never seen before. She'd also put on stockings and make-up, though most of the other women clearly had not made any special effort over their appearance. One of the volunteers told me during the afternoon that Mrs Williams had remarked to her that the club afternoon was the peak of her week, and what else did she have to dress up for? One or two of the other women asked her mockingly who the man was she was meeting, or what her old man would say if he could see her, but there wasn't any nastiness in the remarks. In fact, many of the women seemed rather impressed, and, in front of Mrs Etchells and Mrs Harding, I made a point of complimenting her on how well the dress suited her (Wives' Club).

Tactical goals for group work

This kind of discussion of purposes can, however, be very unreal. On the whole, it probably produces statements about what social workers would *like* to achieve, or would like others to believe they are achieving. In effect, when the question is posed: What is your purpose? the person most involved—in this case, the social worker—is likely to give the answer he feels is expected of him.

Probably more important in practice, therefore, are those short-term objectives which are actually at work in a practitioner's day-to-day activities. What lies behind the social worker's tactical decision to add group work to his normal casework approach? What specifically does he think might result from adopting this somewhat different course of action? Why, in fact, do social workers feel that group experience might help them to be more helpful to their clients? No exact or confident answers to these questions can be given. However, such a tactic might be adopted for a number of different reasons and these often seem to include:

1. Tackling practical and material problems faced by clients

The private, practical, day-to-day problems faced privately by individual clients often have a striking similarity: they constitute recurring, common themes, and can produce continuing and exhausting pressures and anxiety. Young 'unsupported' women—prisoners' wives, unmarried mothers, women divorced or separated from their husbands—might spend almost all their waking hours child-minding. The children of these families, and many others, might be almost entirely cut off from each other, or from any other children of the same age. The women themselves, or perhaps quite a different category of person, such as men who are involuntarily unemployed, might be unaware of their welfare or legal rights, or unable on their own to achieve these or to find a job. Teenagers might be illiterate, prospective adoptive parents nervous about caring for a child, prisoners unsure of the procedures involved in getting parole and anxious about family or employment problems after release.

In general, such problems are very frequently borne alone by the individuals concerned. If, however, they could act together, they might tackle their problems much more effectively. Thus, the purpose of such a group might be stated, both by the social worker and the client, in quite limited and pragmatic terms: to give mothers a chance to discover how other mothers in their position get by, and to meet speakers from the FPA, DHSS, etc; or to inform people of their rights; or to impart some basic child care skills to adoptive parents; and so on.

In these situations, the worker may concentrate only incidentally, if at all, on more deep-seated or long-term emotional and personal needs. And only incidentally may he make use of the more subtle interactional processes which are generated when individuals come together in a group. Thus, for example, the unsupported mothers' needs for a greater sense of personal achievement may be a very low priority. And so, too, may be their potential for initiating and organising more varied and demanding group activities for themselves or others. And so, the playgroup which they themselves could run for their children, or the social club they could establish for unsupported mothers generally in their neighbourhood, may never rate very serious attention by the worker. His focus will remain almost entirely on dealing with immediate and pressing practical problems which, to that point, each of his clients has been used to bearing alone. This, for him, constitutes a goal for the group which is quite adequate in itself.

2. *Developing recreational interests and skills* Closely related to this aim may be one focused primarily on developing individuals' leisure-time interests and skills. Here, the emphasis is shifted from clients' practical problems in the 'occupational' sphere of their lives to their 'recreational' problems. Practice is then designed to help them (collectively again) to meet some of these non-work needs.

In part, this goal may imply that from time to time clients should be distracted from the pressures they feel in the 'work' sphere by being given personally absorbing and socially acceptable 'passtimes', in the almost literal sense of the term such as playing tabletennis and chess competitions. More positively, it may mean providing some fulfilling and expressive experiences for individuals who normally lead very monotonous lives and who are most commonly treated as objects, not people.

In either case, the clear, operational purpose of the group is to complete some quite concrete leisure task, such as building a canoe, sewing a dress, or going on a trip to the seaside. In the process, the practical skills to complete these tasks effectively will be taught because, in the context of the tasks in hand, they are essential. And concern with 'ulterior' purposes, such as meeting individuals' emotional needs or supporting the social networks produced by the group, will occur only incidentally. As in groups preoccupied primarily with 'occupational' problems, the focus will be on what the group is doing rather than on how it is doing it—on content rather than process. The recreational task will, in effect, become the purpose.

3. *Providing further diagnostic material and/or treatment opportunities for use by a worker outside the group situation* Many social workers will undoubtedly dissociate themselves strongly from the relatively narrow task focus of the objectives outlined so far. They will say that they are concerned always with how clients relate and feel, and not just with the 'work'—whether occupational or recreational—which they must tackle. Because their preoccupation is with 'whole people', they will try to see every concrete group task—whether it be petitioning the local authority, claiming benefit, drinking tea and chatting, making dresses or learning how to read—as a potential medium for meeting clients' more personal, if less tangible, expectations and demands.

Social workers may, on this, protest too much. They, it would seem, are as liable as anyone else to get caught up in the task in hand and to consider only retrospectively what it has meant to the human beings involved in it. This would seem to be especially likely when they move into group work situations, whose human complexity and fluidity may surprise and baffle them. For the case-work-trained social worker, in fact, questions like : How good is the canoe we have made? How well do the mothers sew? How accurately do these foster parents understand the functions of my agency? may begin to acquire an unexpectedly important place in their thinking.

Social workers may also, one should add, protest unnecessarily— or at least with unnecessary vehemence—about their concern for 'people' as against 'things'. Even for social workers, there is nothing inherently shameful in adopting a largely task-focused approach. The overwhelming and immediate practical problems which clients have to face are at least as deserving of skilled social work help as are the more impressive—and elusive—psycho-social and emotional difficulties. Though, for the social workers, the latter may have a higher priority, it is doubtful if they always do so for most clients.

Even where the social worker's orientation towards intrapersonal and interpersonal matters is strong, however, he will not necessarily expect the pay-off to be within the group itself. He may in fact see this interaction primarily as a feeding ground for his relations with clients *outside* the group's meetings and boundaries, and especially in the casework situations in which he more normally meets clients.

And so, when the social worker is asked what value he sees in group work, he may in effect reply : 'It improves my casework.' What he may actually say is : 'It helps clients and worker to understand and trust each other better'; or 'The client comes to see the worker in a more informal way'; or 'Seeing a client in a group enables me to clarify what I should do when I next interview him or her'; or 'Experience in a group makes a client much more relaxed and responsive in the casework situation'. The implication here is clearly that group work does enable the social worker to help clients with social and emotional, as well as practical, problems. But apparently, it does so mainly by improving the social work done beyond the group. Group work by this criterion is merely a useful support for casework, where, still, the 'real' social work is done.

4. *Releasing tensions and anxieties* When group experience *is* seen as having importance in its own right, it may be largely because of the cathartic qualities which are attributed to it. In other words, a social worker, by bringing a number of unrelated individuals together, or by influencing their existing interactions, may get them to release tensions, anxieties and similar feelings which would otherwise remain buried.

The underlying assumption here is that, in private, individuals often hold themselves in check, thereby allowing strong emotions to build up inside themselves. Such people may even exaggerate how serious the problems are which are producing those feelings, so that all perspective is lost and the feelings themselves build up still further. By meeting such clients in a group, a worker may be able to use the presence of others as a trigger. What has previously been inhibited is then released, most frequently probably in talk, but also sometimes, perhaps, in energetic or expressive physical action. This latter might take the form merely of forceful gesticulation and other non-verbal behaviour. But it might also occur via games-playing, more controlled bodily movement (such as dance) or artistic activity (see Chapter 6). The worker may describe this process in quite concrete and direct terms : 'The afternoon of tea-drinking sessions gets the mothers out of the house and away from their kids, and lets them leave their problems behind for a change'; or 'The camping expeditions really take the boys out of themselves and bring them back refreshed'; or 'The adoptive parents talked about their fears and regrets, and obviously felt relieved for having done so'. Beneath all such statements seems to be the belief that clients can, or should, join groups in order to purge themselves of a great many feelings which would otherwise remain bottled up.

5. *Achieving some identity with others, and especially those in a similar situation to oneself*   This cathartic purpose for group work may at times, of course, be of great significance, especially when radical alterations in a person's situation are going to be difficult to achieve. However, it will often have only short-term effects: even if some underlying feelings are released, the problems producing them may remain substantially unchanged. Such a purpose is thus likely to be negative in effect, since it focuses primarily on 'empty-ing' the individual of a certain amount of distressing or inhibiting emotion. It does not necessarily fill the gap thus created with any-thing more constructive, such as knowledge about how to deal with the underlying problems, or motivation to act on this know-ledge once it has been acquired.

On the whole, most social workers seem to hope that they can help clients to make more permanent and positive gains in their lives, or at least feel that such gains are possible. In effect, they will wish to help clients beyond the reaction: 'It now seems safe to let off steam in front of these others', at least to the response: 'I can begin to share a little of my "real" self with these others', and even to the conclusion: 'We're a little alike, me and these others. We might even trust each other and begin to do some things together'.

What these more positive reactions imply are the beginnings of a sense of identity with some fellow human beings. For the person concerned, features of the lives and personalities of these others ring echoes in his own existence, and help him to communicate back to them (by word or deed) at least a little of his own feeling. It may be the quite deliberate purpose of group work to foster such a sense of identity as an end in itself. For, such reciprocated belonging, such inter-dependence, can be extremely therapeutic for those who are otherwise alone, and can bring many practical gains which, for the individual in isolation, would always be out of reach.

6. *Achieving change in individuals' self-image, attitudes, behaviour and/or personal circumstances outside the group situation*   In some cases, however, social workers may indeed want, or be able, to pursue much more far-reaching and permanent changes in clients and their circumstances. And the manifestation of many of these changes may be sought *outside* the social work situation *per se*, and in particular outside the group. What is achieved solely within a group, whether it be practical, emotional or social, may thus be welcome and helpful. But it may be seen as insufficient in itself.

Only quite extensive and lasting alterations in people or situations may seem to justify social work intervention.

Such changes, of course, are not easily attained, even when they are ethically justified. Social workers who are too free with their claims, or even their statements of intent, on this score are liable very rapidly to lose touch with the realities of their job. What is particularly clear is that much of this type of change cannot be accomplished by individuals acting singly and in isolation. Even when a client has a supporting group away from the social work situation (such as his family or his peers), such change may still not occur. If these 'significant others' are unaware of, or indifferent to, the social work help he is receiving, they may fail to reinforce the changes it is trying to initiate. Where the outside associations are actively hostile to such help, or where strong economic or institutional pressures are opposing it, change of any importance will probably be beyond his reach.

Individuals (clients and others) therefore may need repeated confirmation of their intentions by others whom they value. And so, group experience introduced as part of their total social work experience can sometimes be crucial. However, this implies that the social worker will need to do more than simply work with clients individually *in* groups. It means also that he must work with clients *through* groups—that is, through the collective intellectual and emotional pressures and bonds which a group can produce.

The underlying assumption once again, therefore, is that *other clients*, and not just the worker himself, may do something to modify an individual's feelings about himself, or his attitudes to others. They may even help to alter facets of that individual's behaviour, or perhaps even of his personal and material circumstances outside the group. Not only might clients act together, therefore. They might also create conditions which ultimately strengthen individuals for independent action outside the group. This might be expressed as: 'Getting the men involved in the community'; or 'Changing attitudes to authority'; or 'Teaching new social skills'; or 'Improving the self-image of underachieving boys with an unstimulating life experience'; or as 'Seeking out latent talent'.

The implication in each case, however, is that clients might sometimes be able to achieve change, for themselves and in their everyday lives, which the worker, acting directly on them or on their behalf, could never achieve.

The caseworker's underlying bias

The categorisation of aims just outlined does not, of course, cover all possible aims. Nor is it meant to imply that each aim is in some way complete in itself and separate from all the others. A social worker may, for example, try to impart outdoor activity skills to clients so that they may be, in his eyes anyway, more constructively and enjoyably involved in their leisure. But he may also, and at the same time, consciously try to use their interaction and identity with each other to change attitudes dangerous to themselves and others. Or again, he may hope that a group of overburdened mothers, while organising play opportunities for their children, will simultaneously relieve some of their own immediate tensions. And he may also encourage them to develop sufficient dynamic over the longer term, both individually and collectively, to deal more effectively with officials who influence or control their lives.

In fact, categorising the possible aims of group work in this way is not intended to suggest that there is some ideal expression or combination of purposes to which all practice—and especially group work practice—should be directed. Rather, it is meant to encourage social workers using, or thinking of using, groups to ask themselves the question: What *extra* or *special* results do I assume might stem from this particular form of work with clients? What, in other words, might the tactical advantages of the method be?

And so, what the above categorisation highlights is the fact that social workers might think of the extra benefits provided by group work in one, of two, general ways. On the other hand, they might see it as a tactic largely or only intended to *support* casework, which is seen as the main method through which social work achieves its primary purposes. Group experience is then looked upon simply as helping individuals to more practical resources, or more recreational or emotional outlets or to increased motivation, *so that they can use the one-to-one situation more effectively*. Or it may be expected to provide caseworkers with information and insights into the individual client and his situation which they would not otherwise have.

Alternatively (or perhaps additionally) a worker may regard group work as a tactic which, *in its own right*, provides a social work service. In this case he will expect the group to give individuals new relationships which they value and which they can use for their own benefit, on the spot, at the point of their actual involvement in them. His aim will be to ensure that *group membership in itself is a force for change.*

Again, these points of view are not mutually exclusive. And neither can be said to have an all-time, any-situation validity. Nonetheless, not all workers will hold to each equally firmly. Indeed, given that most social workers in Britain today see themselves first and foremost as caseworkers, the chances are that they will emphasise the former—the view that group work merely supports the casework method. And, though this is not a view to be scorned, it undoubtedly has its limitations. It will be the burden of the next chapter—in fact, it is an underlying assumption of this whole book—that it is the second perspective which will produce the greatest benefits from group work. If the social worker is alive to the possibilities and is capable of exploiting them, he may be able to use the group as a means with powerful *intrinsic* potential for rendering help to clients.

A special problem of group work: confidentiality

By attempting to place group work as firmly as possible within the mainstream of social work practice, this book clearly implies that the purpose and ethics which guide casework action can in general be expected to guide action in group situations, too. Thus, such basic social work principles as 'self-determination' and 'non-judgmental attitudes', for example, in so far as they are definable and can be made operational, can be said to apply to group work no less than they do to casework.

However, one basic social work principle which in practice may need some reinterpretation for the group work method is that of 'confidentiality'. The conventional view of this is probably best summed up in the British Association of Social Workers' Discussion Paper No. 2. *A Code of Ethics for Social Work* (1972, para. 3.3.12):

> I respect privacy and confidential material about clients gained in my relationship with them or others. I will divulge such material only with the client's consent or in the following circumstances, without his consent:
>> Where there is evidence of serious danger to the client, the worker, other persons or the community; in other exceptional circumstances where, in my professional judgment it seems reasonable and justified.
> If I divulge material in these circumstances I will inform the client as soon as possible. In all such cases I will do my utmost to protect the client against damage to his own interests.

49

In practice, the range of exceptions to this basic principle does often seem to be wider than is apparently admitted here. Thus, discussions which reveal confidential information do seem to occur regularly with colleagues inside an agency, and also often with workers in other, related agencies. When taken together, these can produce a substantial number of breaches of the basic principle.

Nonetheless, the principle itself remains central to most social work thinking and to much social work practice. And in its present form it is often applied uncritically to the group work situation (see, for example, Matthews, 1966, pp. 117-18). But it may often seem to present a serious problem to the caseworker undertaking work in a group. For, in this relatively public situation, what the social worker may find—or fear—is that group members' respect for such confidences is not matched by his own. Indeed, the social worker's very definition of what constitutes confidential material may not be accepted by clients. And so, even where it is agreed within a group that confidences will be protected, breaches of the principle may still occur. Group members may fail to recognise privileged information when they meet it.

It is probably for this reason more than any other that many social workers fear that group experience may damage rather than help clients. They apparently picture a situation in which a client releases a flood of very intimate and personal detail about his life. Because the confidentiality principle cannot be made to stick, they worry that this information will then be used in a very exploitive way, inside and outside the group, by other group members.

Once again, it has to be admitted that such fears are not entirely groundless:

By this time, the girls had their hands covered in flour, and were pounding away at the dough. Suddenly, Judy asked: 'Eh, where's Fran?' No-one answered, and in fact, after a moment's silence Jenny began to talk about cookery lessons at her last school. This went on for quite some time, and was followed by a lot of activity as they rolled the pastry and tried to lift it into the pie-tins. Eventually, though, I was able to ask, in as matter-of-fact voice as I could summon up: 'Where is Fran, by the way?' Again the silence, this time tinged with some sort of feeling (embarrassment? suspicion? hostility?). Only much later did Ellen admit that Fran had been subject to a whispering/rumour campaign all week, the gist of which was that she was a prostitute and went with anyone. It began after last week's meeting, and she had apparently sworn she had finished with the group for good (Community Home Girls' Group).

The risks to individuals in such situations are undoubtedly very real. In defence, one can perhaps only repeat an argument used previously—that all human-relations practice contains some risks, whether it occurs in one-to-one situations, in small groups or in larger groups, or in institutional settings. And one can also stress again that some of these risks may not actually arise out of the group work situations which social workers actually meet. They may stem more from the vivid imagination of workers who are not yet confident in such situations.

But it is important also to add that part at least of the problem may originate from a definition of confidentiality which is inappropriate (at least in part), or unnecessarily rigid. Thus, the extensive definition offered by the British Association of Social Work (1971) purports to be concerned with confidentiality in social work as a whole. And yet, repeatedly, it refers to casework and to the one-to-one interview as if these were synonymous with the social work process as a whole. It claims, for example (para. 1.5), that 'the chief means by which the service of the agency becomes available is through the relationship established between worker and client', and so, totally ignores the service which agencies do, or might, render by facilitating and nurturing *client-client* relationships. Later in the same paragraph, it refers to the social worker's share in highly personal and emotionally charged information in social work *interviews*. And in paragraph 2.1 it talks of the *casework* record and in paragraph 3.5 of casework files.

And yet, social work—especially post-Seebohm, and following the 1969 Children and Young Persons Act and the 1972 Criminal Justice Act—involves much more than one-to-one casework interviews and intensive worker-client relationships. Increasingly important and common is work focusing on *mutual* aid and *community* activity, and so on relationships *between and among* and not just *with* clients. Any current definition of confidentiality in social work must surely reflect these changes, and may in consequence require some radical modifications of the definitions handed down uncritically from a previous era of practice.

It goes without saying, of course, that in an age of computers, data banks and mass media intrusions into personal privacy, the clients' perspective on confidentiality will need to be very fully safeguarded. However, this is not by any means the same as saying that only the worker knows what constitutes confidential material. Indeed, research (see, for example, Mayer and Timms, 1970) is already suggesting that, when looked at from the client's viewpoint, confidentiality can take on a very different meaning from that given to it by the worker, even in the casework interview. For, the client may never realise that the worker intends to keep the content of their conversations strictly to himself. Indeed, far from wanting him to act in such a precious way, the clients may actually expect that the worker *will* actively use the information he has been given once the interview is over. Why else, many clients seem in effect to ask, should I tell him in the first place if all he's going to do is sit on what he knows? What is the use of a wife complaining to a social worker about her husband, or a mother about her teenage daughter, or one neighbour about another, if the social worker does not then act on what he has been told, directly, with the people involved?

Information divulged in a group may of course be introduced with exactly the same motive except that other clients, as well as the worker, may be seen as potential, or actual, allies. This indeed becomes even more likely when one considers the standards which may be taken for granted by many clients. For, in many closed institutions, neighbourhoods, friendship groups, and so on, quite personal and highly charged information circulates freely— and, what is more, is expected to do so. At the very least, a silent conspiracy may be at work among all the parties involved, that it should do so.

The social worker, of course, in shocked or superior tones, may call many such exchanges 'gossip', 'rumour', or 'the grapevine', and steadfastly refuse to listen to them. And often he will be right, because their accuracy is questionable and the social worker's own integrity may be damaged by too close an involvement with them. Nonetheless, such exchanges can be very helpful to the social work process, at least as a source of information and also as a means of getting messages through to elusive individuals. More to the point in the present context, they may also represent *the clients'* operational definition of confidentiality. This definition is not self-evidently inferior in all circumstances to that of the social work profession, is bound to intrude at times and in influential ways into the group work situation, and can often prove extremely constructive.

Suddenly, in the middle of the discussion, Fred asked: 'What do we expect we'll be doing when we're 65?' This, understandably, brought a long silence, which seemed to me to be deeply reflective. Reg broke it, by murmuring softly: 'Old and broke, I s'pose', though the irony was clearly not intended to get a laugh. Jamie then added: 'If I'm alive at all', and this somehow seemed to release Alf, who began to say very quietly, 'Well, of course, I'm homosexual, and s'pose I always will be. If I die peacefully in my bed like my grandma did, I'll be satisfied. She was 80 when she died.' 'Yes, I'd hate to linger and die in pain,' Bill said and Sammy agreed. No-one even commented on Alf's homosexuality, though, as far as I know, it was the first time anyone (including the officers) knew anything about it (Day Treatment Centre).

Such a highly pragmatic conception of confidentiality may not, however, be acceptable to the social worker. He will then presumably go on applying the strict view of confidentiality which he believes is correct, and as, for example, Konopka (1972, p. 89) and Northen (1969, p. 124), suggest, he should try also to get other group members to do the same. Information communicated to him by clients outside the group will thus not be revealed within the group, even though, once he possesses this extra knowledge, the worker may adjust his own responses. Information emerging within the group will not be discussed privately with any group members other than the person who reveals it. Where individuals seem to be revealing too much, or other individuals seem to be taking advantage of what has come out, the worker will, quite directively perhaps, confine behaviour within acceptable limits. And at regular intervals, and especially at the very beginning of his association with a group, the worker will make explicit what he sees the rules of confidentiality to be.

In the end, however, the worker's freedom of choice may be very restricted. If he does not want to work within situations which are entirely worker-constructed and worker-dominated, some interaction between his own and his clients' conceptions of confidentiality is bound to occur, and a working agreement reached. Indeed, if he wants to use the fluidity and mutuality of group encounters to help his clients, it is doubtful if he can afford to control a group's structure so completely. At least partial accommodation on this, as on so many other issues, may therefore be essential.

The confidentiality ethic in social work was never intended to be an end in itself. It was designed, one presumes, to assure clients that they might trust social workers—to ensure that workers used personal information passed to them, in ways which *clients* recognised as proper. The principle of confidentiality—or anything else in professional practice—could easily rigidify to the point where it actually gets in the way of such an outcome, without in any real sense protecting the client from an invasion of privacy. A major swing to group work by social workers may, at least where confidentiality is concerned, prevent such an outcome.

In concluding this section, one further point would seem worth making. What is at stake here, it is being suggested, is the respect social workers show for the private nature of the information entrusted to them. In the end, this is not primarily a matter of observing some traditional rule handed down as part of a professional code. It is a matter of personal sensitivity to what is appropriate for a particular individual at a particular moment. The guideline normally is not What is laid down as correct? but What would be most helpful to this human being? As group work experience reveals time and again, social workers have no premium of such sensitivity, and social work clients are certainly not totally bereft of it. They, often as quickly and accurately as the social worker, will recognise what is needed and will act accordingly. Perhaps that is why the problem of preserving confidences within a group can so often seem much less pressing in practice than it does in theory.

The limitations of group work

Merely to raise such dilemmas, however, is to make clear that, for all its advantages and potentialities, group work is no panacea. In fact, at this particular moment in social work's evolution, it seems especially important to recognise that it has some quite definite drawbacks.

One of the greatest of these is undoubtedly that group work, because it is often seen as a threat to established ways of working, and because understanding of it and expertise in it are still quite limited, is likely to be much less effective than it should or could be. The personal preferences, abilities and sense of security of a worker are after all always important factors in carrying out the tasks of social work. Group work, simply by being strange to so many workers, is almost bound to touch these personal elements of practice in sensitive places, at least initially.

Indeed, the fact that so far, social work has relied so heavily on the casework interview probably means that it has recruited people who professionally are much more at ease in one-to-one situations and who are much more convinced about their value. Social workers who prefer, and who are comfortable in, groups may therefore be comparatively rare—a possibility examined at greater length in the final chapter.

This, for group work, may have two adverse effects. First, it can mean an external environment for group work practice, in agencies and among colleagues, which is unsympathetic, indifferent or, at best, mildly tolerant. And second, it can mean that many of the attempts by social workers to work with groups are inadequately prepared and so go off at half-cock. Moreover, these two factors may continually reinforce each other. Lack of positive support from superiors and colleagues may weaken group workers' confidence and motivation, and so almost ensure failure or only limited success. And these poor examples of the method in practice may only confirm the sceptics in their scepticism.

There are, however, other disadvantages, or at least difficulties, in group work which are more intrinsic to it as a method. Perhaps the most serious is that, almost by definition, it may increase the stigma attached to being a client and increase clients' separation from individuals and groups who do not share their special circumstances and problems. It was suggested earlier that individuals in a group can gain a great deal if to some extent they are, and can come to feel, like their fellow group members. For the physically handicapped, the isolated or unsupported mother, the friendless child or adolescent, the powerless welfare claimant or the persistent petty offender—for all of these, and many others, the discovery that they are not alone, or that they are not mad because they feel as they do, or that they are not totally unacceptable to other people, can be very reassuring.

However, these gains do largely depend on these special 'types' of people coming together, for some of their time at least, as a group quite separate from the non-special—that is, the 'normal'— people around them. This is liable to confirm their labelled status, and so strengthen their sense of being different and make it more difficult for them to establish themselves in situations of ordinary everyday social intercourse. If a group does not at least provide a bridge to these outside situations, then it is doubtful if in the long run it is achieving its purpose. That is why the ultimate validation for group work cannot be how people feel about, or perform within, such a group. It can only be seen as how they feel and perform outside it.

Closely related to this risk is the possibility that a group may become, not just inward-looking, but extremely *group* focused. The concern of some of the individuals in the group may be increasingly for the group, its cohesion, its control over its members, its reputation. These introspective considerations may even become so powerful that individuals and their welfare are sacrificed to them. A group evolving in this way is clearly acting in ways diametrically opposed to the values and ethics which, it was suggested earlier, need to guide all social work practice. Yet this is undoubtedly a potential disadvantage, inherent in the very advantages of group work. As individuals discover some common goals and a sense of identity, they may come to value this above all else. And, at that point, they may begin to make the group's requirements, and not the requirements of individuals, ends in themselves.

All this, of course, is simply another way of saying that 'good' does not emerge inevitably when individuals meet in a group any more than it does than when they are encountered in a one-to-one interview situation. The 'good' has to be worked for, by clients and also by the worker.

5

The processes of interaction

From time to time, when I collect my young son from school, I hold rambling conversations with him about his day's experience. It was only after several of these—indeed, it was only while writing this chapter—that I realised that, to prompt him, I would invariably ask: 'What did you do today, Neil?' or 'Did you paint?' or 'What did you have for dinner?' Questions like 'Who did you play with?' or 'Who painted with you?' or 'Who did you sit next to at dinner?' seemed somehow to occur to me much less spontaneously.

Here, perhaps, is an illustration of how, when human interaction is considered, we so often think primarily in terms of 'doing'—talking, painting, playing, eating, or perhaps sewing or canoe-building, petitioning or community serving. Yet human beings in interaction can also be thought of simply as 'being', in the sense that through such interaction individuals express their inner, spontaneous needs and feelings, both about themselves and also about those to whom they are relating. Viewed from this stand-point, situations of interaction can be seen as microscopic exchanges. Investments are then made in, and through, other personalities, and rewards are sought and embodied in a social and emotional currency.

Here, spelt out rather more directly than previously, is a key assumption which has underpinned all that has been written in this book so far. The point has now been reached when some of the detail of this implicit, conceptual and theoretical framework needs to be explained rather more fully.

The self as a social product

Basic to this framework is a definition of 'the individual' which especially emphasises his or her interdependence with others. It acknowledges that 'core' features of the person—capacities, propensities, traits—will exist and persist. And it recognises that these will often remain untouched by the person's surrounding environment, that they will strongly influence his behaviour, and that they need to be recognised and valued by any 'helping' agent.

Yet an interactionist perspective assumes that fixed, core features of personality will by no means account for everything that one individual sees of another within a group situation. For the 'self' is also inward-looking and reflexive. Unlike other animals, human beings can *describe* the facts of their own personality as they perceive them. That is, they can say that they are six feet tall, moody, good with figures and so on. And, even more significant, they can also *evaluate* these facts, or (to use the phraseology of an earlier chapter) attach *meanings* to the facts and judge them as good or bad, desirable or undesirable. This capacity for self-perception, self-analysis and self-criticism is vital, above all because time and time again it moves individuals to *action*—it affects what they actually do, and how they actually relate to others. This active responsiveness to self thus also produces an active responsiveness to the social environment, which in turn does much to determine how any individual self is presented to others at any moment in time.

Thus a person's self-image and self-expectations can go far in deciding how he or she actually behaves. Moreover, such a view of self clearly cannot be created in isolation from others. The individual only knows how to describe some of the key features of his own person and then how to evaluate those, because of the feedback he has received on these things from others. The interaction, therefore, between

(a) the 'core' person;
(b) his image, expectations and evaluations of himself;
(c) other people's image, expectations and evaluations of him;
(d) and the image and expectations which *he believes* others have of him, helps to create, and then constantly to some degree to re-create, what we call in brief, 'the self'. Rather than being some in-built and untouchable entity, therefore, the self needs to be seen as 'a product of a person's interaction with others ... a social product' (Hargreaves, 1972, p. 9).

It is important to note, however, that what occurs is not merely the *release* by one person of what is special and already embedded in another. Rather, interaction among human beings actually helps to *define* and *create* the characteristics of the self which are unique or highly individual. Thus, the individual is actually *constructed* in relationships with others, so that 'the self arises from the social

experience of interacting with others' (Hargreaves, 1972, p. 11).
'Being' thus means 'being in relation with others'—that is:
(a) reacting to them;
(b) evoking their reactions to me;
(c) organising these reactions in a way I can understand; and
(d) internalising at least some of this feedback until it actually
becomes 'me'.
To a large extent, therefore, individuals 'are' what they permit and
encourage others—and especially 'significant others', like parents,
teachers and perhaps social workers—to inform them they are.

Another way of describing these expectations and self-expectations is to say that the 'self' of an individual is an accumulation
or configuration of the roles which he or she is required to play
within each social situation he enters. To some extent, the individual
will both create these expectations initially and also re-mould them
by the way he actually acts them out once he is within the situation.
Nonetheless, what others see of his behaviour may, to a significant
degree, be his personal performance of the role or roles 'allocated'
to him by others—a particular presentation of himself designed
to meet the expectations then operating. He, or an outsider, may
refer to some of this role-playing as his 'real' self. And by this, they
will normally mean that he is performing in roles—that is, according to expectations/self-expectations—which he is able to fulfil
most spontaneously and comfortably. However, the self which
emerges in other less 'natural' ways may be no less 'real': it may
merely be a view of the person picked up while he is trying on
other, less well-fitting and less comfortable roles.

This individual movement into and out of roles defined within,
and by, group interaction can often be seen most clearly in the
way 'leadership' is exercised. At one time, the search for the
essential personal qualities of a leader was all absorbing. Leadership,
it was implied, is embedded in the individual.

Though this view does to some extent still persist, much greater
attention is now paid to leadership as a product and a function of
a particular group situation. Group members, it is recognised, need
certain types of contribution from each other—technical, social,
emotional and so on—to achieve their shared goals. In order to
ensure this contribution is made, they are willing to give up a
degree of personal freedom to the individual or individuals capable
of making it. If these individuals agree to contribute in the necessary
way, they are encouraged and/or permitted to lead.

Of course, the process which actually occurs is rarely, if ever,
as rational or logical as this. Nonetheless, this analysis illustrates
the two main points being made in this context. First, a 'leader'

is created by members of a group in interaction, and not solely by the characteristics of a single individual. And second, an individual may therefore move into and out of the role of leader— i.e. may present different versions of his 'self'—as the group's requirements, and so their expectations of him and of each other, change. A 'self' is rarely, if ever, permanently controlling, directing, initiating—that is, leading. Some of its presentations and formulations may be of this kind as other individuals expect and require it. But other such presentations, at other times and in other circumstances, may cast it in a very different role.

An interactionist perspective in practice

This exposition of the self and of the expectations which lead to shifting versions of it, is not introduced here merely as an academic diversion. For the practitioner, it has some major implications. In particular, it suggests that the human interactions in which a practitioner intervenes can be extremely dynamic *now* and are therefore still capable of significant further movement. Individuals will, of course, be firmly set in many important respects, and will be strongly influenced today by the residue within their personalities of past experience and events. But personality is not solely a storage container for such residue. It is also a constantly reacting organism. And practitioners can choose to concentrate on those substantial features of the self which, in order to meet the expectations and self-expectations of a particular time and of particular circumstances, are being presented in a particular way, here and now. By trying to modify some of those features which are special to the way interaction is currently organised and shaped, the practitioner may thus make a significant contribution to the renewal of 'self', and so to individual development.

It does not of course require a formal group meeting to set these interactions of self and situations in motion. A one-to-one interview undoubtedly induces them also (Ashton, 1972, p. 14):

> In a process of mental feed-back, each person in an interview is consciously or unconsciously trying to assess what impression he is making on another. He is trying to gauge how his image looks when seen in the mirror of the other's judgement. The responses of the other may be quite different from expectations, leading to revaluation and reorientation of expressive behaviour.

Thus, in a casework interview, as in any other social encounter, the underlying self-images and self-expectations, and the actual presentations of 'self' are not established for all time. The 'self' of both the client and the worker as perceived in the interview could—indeed almost certainly will—be re-presented in most unexpected, even startling, ways in other arenas of interaction, like, for example, a small group. Some of the case material already included in this book (see, for example, pp. 37 and 41) illustrate this point very clearly.

Thus, once again we can see that 'group' needs to be conceived very flexibly indeed. And, for the social work 'client', it must include the social work agency itself, since, it is this agency which has attached the label 'client' in the first place, and so has set some key expectations, and self-expectations, for that individual. In other words, within that arena of interaction we call a social work agency, client 'selves' are undoubtedly re-created to some degree, perhaps especially by the social worker. And so what the client *as client* 'is'—his re-presentation of himself—results not only from what his infancy and childhood, his parents, teachers, neighbours and friends have made him. It stems also, and perhaps in important ways, from how he is perceived and labelled by the social worker in the social work situation itself and then from the expectations which flow from these perceptions and labels. The moment the client incorporates part or all of this definition of his self into his person, then what the social worker sees of 'him' will have been significantly affected by what *the social worker* has contributed to the interaction. And, even when the client refuses to accept the definition accorded to him, his presentation of self, as this is perceived by the worker, will still be affected, since it is at those moments, or in those cases, that his person may be described as 'resistant' or 'apathetic' or 'hostile'. In these ways, a complicated circular process of expectation and self-fulfilling prophecy, will almost certainly have been initiated.

What is now being described in more detail, therefore, is how and why the very parameters within which social work operates can, in very practical ways, distort the helping process, by seriously affecting the interaction in which client and social worker are involved. For, attaching the label 'client' to an individual is not a neutrally descriptive *event*, complete in itself and without continuing repercussions. It is a *process*. It goes on developing and conveying expectations that the labeller has of the person labelled. The expectations touch among other things, the labelled person's status in relation to the labeller, the labelled person's anticipated and required behaviour towards the labeller, the labelled person's self-image, and the labelled person's capacities for autonomous action when the labeller—the social worker—is not present. All this may, of course, be helpful to 'the client'. But it may not be.

And it can in no way be said to sum up his whole potential, or actual, self-presentation.

This of course has very wide-ranging practical implications. It affects not just the social worker as group worker, but the social worker *per se*. Or, put in another way, it again requires that the cast of mind of the group worker be applied to all the situations in which the social worker finds himself—and not just to those situations in which 'set-piece' groups can be identified.

All this, of course, greatly oversimplifies what can in reality take place. An individual throughout life may acquire a very firm self-image and some deeply entrenched self-expectations which often lead him, deliberately almost, into situations in which these will be confirmed and reinforced. Indeed, this may happen even though, for the person concerned, the roles into which these expectations force him are full of pain, conflict, even rejection: to adjust his view and presentation of himself might involve even greater stress.

Moreover, because of this self-perpetuating process, others may come to acquire expectations of the person concerned which lead *them* to confirm him in the roles and self-presentations which he has tended to make his own. The more of his behaviour and interactions that this process affects, the less easily or fully will the person concerned develop. Again, the temptation may be to conclude: this is 'him'. In reality, however, a complicated jigsaw of reciprocated and reinforced expectations may exist whose construction a worker may need to influence and even modify, and which certainly, in his professional capacity, he would often not want simply to confirm.

The 'organisation' of group interaction

How, in practice, a worker might respond to these self-making processes will be discussed in greater detail in Chapter 7. At this point, it is necessary to look much more closely at the main pieces of the jigsaw—at the essential elements of the interaction out of which a particular version of the 'self' emerges—and to see how the pieces fit together.

In Chapter 3 it was suggested that a group might be thought of as an organism whose internal processes were capable of becoming increasingly complex. Such complexity will almost certainly mean that its members become much more interdependent. And this in turn will assume much *organised*—that is, structured and ordered—interaction among otherwise separate and apparently autonomous individuals.

At moments, of course, the structure may be primitive and weak. It may even break down completely, or sub-structures within what is known overall as 'this group' may appear. The structure that does exist may never be overt or concrete in its expression. It may have to be inferred by an outsider, and may remain unrecognised, at least in part, even by the group members themselves.

Nonetheless, for a group's organic growth to occur, individuals must move from being independent of, even alienated from, each other to a position of reciprocated investment in a common present and a partially shared future. And this in turn demands some form of structured or patterned responses, one individual to another. When such responses do exist, even though they may be evaluated as harmful or undesirable, the interaction (the relationships) as well as the tasks (the activities) can be said to have achieved a degree of *organisation*.

What does such organisation involve? Any description of such a complex area of human experience is bound to be oversimple and unreal. However, it seems worth separating the following features:

1. Individual group members may share (or come to share) certain *values*—that is, certain beliefs about what is good and bad, and right and wrong, within and for *the group*. These values may emerge out of experience and evidence, or be based entirely on faith. They may apply very generally also outside the group's immediate operations, or they may be confined strictly to the group members' joint interaction. What is crucial in this context is that the values may be felt to be *shared* by the individuals concerned and applied to their common tasks and interactions inside this group.

2. Out of these shared values, common *goals* may arise which to some degree, group members seek to attain collectively. In other words, individuals may first accept that certain material objects or non-material outcomes (such as winning a game or caring for a neighbour) are good and right. They then in effect agree to make the *achievement* of these objects or outcomes a desirable end which they will move towards together. These shared objectives thus come to embody in practice the values they hold in common, at least in this particular group.

Phil, followed by Mark then sat themselves inside Miss R's car and locked the doors and wound up the windows. They then went through a charade of starting up the engine, putting the car in gear and driving it, head low over the steering wheel, at great speed. They laughed and pointed mockingly as Miss R and I tried to reason with them, and then threaten them, from the outside. They probably couldn't even hear most of what we were saying. Tim, Pete and John stood just a little way away, laughing loudly and making funny remarks, obviously enjoying every moment of our discomfort. The lads seemed absolutely united in their dislike of us as embodiments of authority, and were clearly intent on wringing every ounce of enjoyment for themselves and embarrassment for us out of their temporary advantage (Boys' Camp Group).

Mrs Jones and Mrs Etchells then got into a sharp disagreement about how much use their husbands are to them. Mrs Jones, as always, was loyal to her 'ol' man', in spite of his treatment of her and the kids and his inability to stay out of trouble. He was her husband and that, as far as she was concerned, was enough. Mrs Etchells obviously regards her husband as a nuisance and a drag, and feels a great release every time he goes inside. Though she barely gets enough to live on from 'the assistance', at least it's regular and she knows it's hers, and she isn't worrying all the time that the police are suddenly going to reappear on her doorstep. The two women kept up their argument for quite a time, often laughing at and with each other, and enjoying the accompanying banter of the other women, though neither gave an inch on her personal point of view. Mrs Graham said at the end that they all really enjoyed the discussions and it did them good to 'talk about things' like they did (Wives' Club).

3. However, group members cannot take for granted that every individual will, within the group, actually act on the accepted shared values or pursue the agreed common goals. The behaviour of individual group members may have to be regulated to ensure they actually do act according to the values and in the interest of the goals laid down by the group. Certain rules (or *norms*) of behaviour may therefore have to be established to provide this regulation—that is, to limit individual freedom in the name of collective achievement.

4. These norms will not, however, be accepted automatically by group members. They may on occasions have to be backed up, in particular by *sanctions*, which will either impel or attract individuals into an at least minimum degree of conformity. These sanctions may therefore take the form either of punishments for failure to conform, or of rewards for doing so adequately or especially well.

Mr Henry then called for a vote on the proposition which had already been put to the committee, and the Chairman (Mr Wright) agreed to this. Mrs Baker complained ('on a point of order') that there had not been enough discussion as it was a very important matter they were deciding. Mr Wright over-ruled her, but Mrs Baker continued to protest, until eventually Mr Henry again suggested to the Chairman that the vote be taken, and that, if Mrs Baker continued to flout the Chairman's rulings, she should be asked to leave the meeting. Mr Wright agreed, and only then did Mrs Baker shut up. She remained sulky and silent for most of the rest of the meeting (Community Action Group).

As I was preparing to put the record on the record-player, Becky tapped me on the shoulder and pointed her head to the corner of the room, where Eric was sitting squat-legged half-facing the wall. I went over, to find him in tears, and then asked generally 'What happened?' Debbie said: 'It was Ray. He called him four-eyes and swore at him.' I looked at Ray, who vehemently denied he had done anything of the sort. Debbie exclaimed angrily: 'Of course you did, you sod. I heard you.' Becky went over and clumsily sat herself very near to Ray, while Jenny murmured from behind me: 'Thump him, Mr C. Really bash him. He's really been asking for it' (Physically Handicapped Adolescent Group).

5. In order actually to pursue shared goals, however, group members must *do* things together—that is, they must undertake certain *tasks*. Where the goals are explicit, the tasks may be very concrete. A football team, to win football matches, must play football; a community action group, to win better housing con-ditions, must petition or picket housing departments or withhold rents. Some goals are less overt—like, for example, giving and receiving social acceptance, or learning how to relate to one's peers. Even these goals may be achieved via quite concrete and explicit tasks, such as playing football or petitioning. But often they are not, since on many occasions they may involve little more than (as in a Wives' Club or a Boys' Camp) sitting around very casually, chatting and drinking tea or beer, against a background of pop music or the television. Nonetheless, such tasks still represent the 'doing' by which individuals seek to move towards their goals.

6. However, even for the simplest of human tasks, a very wide range of intricate, interdependent actions may be demanded. Often, performing all these actions will be beyond the capacities and/or

interests of any single individual. And yet all or most of them may need to be performed by someone if the group's goals are to be achieved and its values expressed in practice. Some division of labour among group members will therefore be almost inevitable, with individuals to some degree taking on specialised functions. It is at this point that expectations may emerge among group members about what any individual will do, about how he or she will behave. Moreover, each individual may come to have certain expectations of himself and his own behaviour within the context of the group's tasks. These expectations and self-expectations may, as we have seen, be constantly measured against how individuals actually *do* behave, and may be modified accordingly. Ultimately, however, they will lead to an allocation and acceptance of certain *roles* in a group which will seek to pattern to some degree individuals' actions within it and towards each other. In some of the case material already quoted, this process may be (even if only faintly) discerned at times. In the Physically Handicapped Adolescent Group, for example, Ray (as persecutor), Eric (as persecuted scapegoat) and Debbie (as defender) seem to be adopting some such patterned responses. So, too, perhaps, in the Wives' Club, is Mrs Jones (as provocateur), as perhaps, also, in the Boys' Camp Group, are Phil (as informal task leader—see pp. 63-4) and Mark (as second in command). And in the Community Action Group, Mr Wright is of course designated, within the group's formal division of labour, as 'Chairman'.

7. This division of labour may have a further effect: it may mean that at any moment in time, an individual group member differs, not only in what he does, but also in his worth to the group, or in what he feels his worth to the group to be. This worth, or feeling of self-worth, may depend also on how wholeheartedly the individual accepts the group's shared values, on how vigorously he pursues its common goals or on how enthusiastically he supports its laid-down norms. As this ranking or *status* may constitute one of the main forms of reward available to loyal and conforming group members, it may represent a key sanction for enforcing group norms. Yet, this cannot be regarded as an absolute rule, since, once an individual has achieved, or feels he has achieved, high status, he may have greater freedom of action, and so more opportunity to overlook group norms, than most other group members. Thus, it would seem that Mrs Williams, almost *because* of her breach of group norms over dress in the Wives' Club (see p. 41) actually gains status. And the same could even be true of Mrs Baker in the Community Action Group (p. 64) as a result of her refusal to accept the chairman's insistence on strict committee

procedure without a fight. Nonetheless, a positive correlation between conformity to group values, goals and norms and the allocation of worth among group members can frequently be expected. Mrs Jones' contribution to the Wives' Club would, it seems, make her highly valued by her fellow group members, while Ray's behaviour in the Physically Handicapped Adolescent Group apparently greatly reduces his status in that group.

8. As these illustrations also suggest to some extent, a hierarchy of status may exist which is related to (though again not necessarily entirely coincident with) a hierarchy of *authority*—that is, a hierarchy of opportunities and rights to direct and control the actions of other group members. An individual may be worth a great deal to the group at any particular moment because of what he contributes to its tasks and how he aids the attainment of group goals. His adherence to group norms may also be high. In this case, he is likely (though not certain) to enjoy some additional privileges, including a right to limit other group members' freedom. The corollary of this is also likely to be true—that, because of their roles and status, certain individuals will have fewer of these opportunities and rights, and so find themselves in a subordinate position in the hierarchy.

These elements of group organisation have been presented in much too mechanistic a way, almost as if each follows the next by inevitable progression. Also, the difficulty of distinguishing them in practice is greatly understated in such a crude description. Many groups, for example, display one or more of these elements— say, a division of labour and so a role structure or an authority hierarchy—only weakly, if at all. Or, ranking and a distribution of authority may occur very early: they may be imposed on a group, or individuals may be known outside the group to other group members and so may bring status (high or low) and influence (strong or weak) with them into the group. What is also true is that the internal meaning of each of the elements of group structure —the meaning each has for any particular group member, may vary considerably. It may also be very different from the meaning attached to them by the detached (external) observer.

Thus, extracting artificially in this way from complicated human experience will always have its limitations. Nonetheless, it can still help the group worker to understand better, and so perhaps to respond more appropriately to, the events he is negotiating. The idea that groups might organise their relationships as well as their activities can at times prove extremely useful.

Formal and informal elements of group organisation

This organisation of group interaction is complicated by a further factor: much of it will not, of course, be made explicit. In some groups—for example, the Community Action Group—much of the structure will, it is true, be embodied in quite concrete forms or in clearly identifiable procedures and people. Taken together, such things as written constitutions, standing orders and designated officers may seem to leave both participant and observer in little doubt about the group's key objectives, norms, sanctions, ascribed roles and so on.

Other groups—like, perhaps, the Day Treatment Centre—may depend much less on constitutions and written rules but may in their own way be equally explicit about their structure. And in still other groups, the organisation of interaction may be even less overt or concrete. Above all, some groups may actually state certain *formal* elements of their organisation and yet simultaneously support other, *informal* elements which remain implicit—as in the Community Action Group, perhaps, where Mr Henry may on many occasions use the chairman's formal authority to establish and exercise his own informal authority and influence. In some such groups—in the Physically Handicapped Adolescent Group, for example, when Debbie and Mr C each in their own way seek to sustain Eric against Ray's attacks (p. 65)—the formal and informal structures may complement each other. But, in others, two alternative and *conflicting* forms of organisation may establish themselves. The informal structure may even ultimately prove to be more acceptable and satisfying to group members than the formal, so that, in practice, the formal structure is reduced to a mere façade. The Boys' Camp Group would seem to experience some such development, however temporary (see p. 63).

Outsiders—amongst whom we may often need to include the social worker—will usually be very aware of the formal and explicit elements of group organisation and seek to relate their behaviour to it. The chairman, team captain or gang leader, the objectives stated explicitly, the rules of procedure laid down and the concrete tasks pursued, may, to the worker, be obvious targets for encouragement or negation.

The informal structure may, however, be harder both to identify and to influence. Yet it may be enormously significant for individual group members because it touches what are, for them, important though perhaps unverbalised expectations and needs. Thus, the role of scapegoat, which social workers may identify very quickly, is never formally designated. Nonetheless, it may be allocated because group members informally mark off someone to carry an individual or collective burden of fear of failure, guilt, anxiety or frustration. And it may be accepted by that person because, whatever the pain it brings, it *is* a role in the group and so, does allocate to that individual some functions, and so some recognition, as a group member.

Many other roles are equally informal in the sense that they are achieved without ever being formally designated or ascribed. Some of these informal roles may involve carrying out tasks which are *instrumental* to achieving the group's stated (that is, formal) goals (see p. 75). These tasks may include such items as organising the group's tea-making or improvised acting or discussion topic, giving or seeking information, co-ordinating or focusing group members' actions, or recording or evaluating what has been done.

Other informal roles may be much more concerned with individuals' on-the-spot *self-expression*, and so may be described as *expressive*. Some of these may be *group-focused*—that is, focused on, say, regulating entry to the group, or encouraging or supporting compromise among conflicting individuals. Others may stem much more from *the need of the individual* who plays them to release personal feelings and attitudes. They may therefore express themselves in actions which block formal work on group tasks directly (as when Ray attacked Eric verbally in the Physically Handicapped Adolescent Group), or indirectly (as when someone from the Community Home Girls' Group, spread rumours about Fran outside the group as a result of what she said about herself inside the group). Such role-taking is not usually formally ascribed, and so must be seen as embodying an influential, but informal, division of labour.

What is true of roles, may be no less true of the other elements of group structure. Norms, for example, may never be formally laid down but they may indicate that swearing is permitted or not permitted; or that exploitation, one group member of another, is allowable or not allowable; or that intimate details about one's personal life may, or may not, be revealed; or that one may, or may not, become overtly enthusiastic about the group's formal tasks. Such rules may in turn be enforced by sanctions which are never formally acknowledged—by scorn, by rejection, even by physical coercion when the rules are broken; or by praise or improved status when they are well observed. And in the case of both the norms and the sanction, what is established informally may directly contradict what the formally approved organisation lays down.

The social worker must of course assume that a group's informal structure may have very great practical significance for him. The seductive pressures and attractions of at least parts of it can be very powerful, especially when group members are highly unself-conscious about their interaction and when the worker is (like many caseworkers) unsure of himself in a group situation. Thus, a group may *say*: We want to become more open in our expression of feeling; or, We want to use our collective strength to improve our housing conditions or to get our welfare or civil rights. But, what if, through its informal structure, it punishes individuals for exposing themselves emotionally in the group, perhaps merely by ignoring them or even by using the information gained to humiliate them? Or if it expends, in fighting internal battles for control of the group itself, energy which is desperately needed for conducting a campaign against the housing department? A group worker who ignores the informal elements of the group's organisation may, in these circumstances, merely disable the group further in its pursuit of its stated, formal goals, or miss valuable opportunities for helping it move closer to those goals.

Stages of group development

Using terms like 'organisation' of group interaction, and formal or informal 'structures' does, however, involve a serious risk. For it implies a much more static view of groups, or of any inter-actional situation, than is ever likely to be found in practice. And, in suggesting such lack of movement, it contradicts a conception of 'group' already strongly emphasised in this book; namely, that of an *organism* capable of developing its internal processes and of remaining constantly dynamic.

The question which now needs to be asked, therefore, is: What, more precisely, does such movement involve? Can any patterns in this movement, be discerned? Does the interaction of initially separate individuals evolve via any steps or stages which are recognisable and even, perhaps, to some degree, recurring and/ or predictable?

A number of attempts have been made to answer this particular question (see, for example, Northen, 1969; Sarri and Galinsky, 1967; Rogers, 1970, Chapter 2; Hartford, 1972, Chapter 3; and the synthesis of some of the most important work in this field, in Douglas, 1970, Chapter 2). A further, very basic framework for conceptualising group development is presented below. At the outset, however, its limitations need to be acknowledged quite explicitly. No model of group development can ever account for all aspects of a group's experience or be helpful in all the group situations a social worker may meet. Nor can any very convincing claims be made for its predictive qualities, since there will always be innumerable variables which make precise statements about the future order and nature of events extremely unreliable.

The framework may for many social workers be limited also because they do not enter a group at the very start of its life. Thus, in practice, the initial stage of group development may have been completed long before the social worker appears on the scene. This will certainly be true of, say, a teenage friendship group, or a 'living' group in a hostel, or of many neighbourhood groups. Also, many such groups, as well as some 'formed' groups, may never go through any final stage, at least while a worker is associated with them.

In the light, also, of the phenomenological view outlined earlier, one further limitation must be admitted: when examined through the eyes of different group members, the same group may simultaneously be at a number of different stages of development. This may apply particularly where group composition changes during the lifetime of a group—for example, once again, in many residential situations, and in many 'social' groups such as wives' and youth clubs and children's playgroups. The perception of the group's stage of evolution by a newcomer, by an old hand and by a near 'graduate' will often differ substantially.

Moreover, at this point it must also be acknowledged that what is primarily being considered here is the 'set-piece' group situation which has certain recognisable boundaries of time, space and personnel. More informal and fluid situations of human interaction may indeed be illuminated by what follows in this section. Nonetheless, the focus is above all on relatively formalised examples of such interaction which an onlooker would recognise as constituting 'a group'.

In spite of all these limitations and qualifications, some understanding of how interaction might evolve over time can be extremely helpful for a social worker—and also, for that matter, for a client too. They may never *know* what is to come. But they may become more aware of what is happening now and of some of the factors motivating it. And they may then be able to plan just a little more appropriately for a variety of possible next steps.

Broadly speaking, then, as a group establishes and organises its internal interaction—its formal and informal structures—to meet the instrumental and expressive tasks with which it is faced, it might be seen or felt to be negotiating any or all of the following stages of development.

71

1. A synchronisation of personalities When two people who already know each other meet in strange circumstances, strains in their relationship can often appear. When the two people concerned are complete strangers, the strains may be even more noticeable. And when the number of strangers rises to three, four or more, the stress each feels may become acute.

In such groups, the symptoms of the discomfort are often very obvious. Silences can be long and frequent. Even when words are exchanged, they may be delivered with little fire or enthusiasm. Indeed, the whole mood may be extremely low-key and tentative, and may be enlivened only by sarcasm or weak jokes. Only if the group allows for non-verbal activity is there likely to be an energetic response, and this may be so frenetic that it seems to be useful mainly as a form of emotional escape or self-protection.

A social worker who is entering a newly formed group will no doubt himself share many of these feelings and reactions. He may therefore take the emotional atmosphere so for granted that he never consciously considers the interactional processes which are combining to produce it. Yet this first meeting of personalities merits careful study. At the extreme, it can make or break a group. Less dramatically, but equally significantly, it can allow a worker, by his initial interventions, to make group members' later experiences in the group much more positive. For, he can help to identify and establish a form of social organisation which (when measured against the group's goals) is constructive, at the expense of those which are not.

What then are the key features of the personal exchanges occurring at this early stage? A major factor in any initial human encounter is, as Michael Argyle (1967) has pointed out, the need of the individuals involved to 'synchronise their social techniques'. If a relationship (or in this case, a network of relationships) is to establish itself, then each participating person must, where necessary, modify his individual style of relating, must adjust it to the style of the other(s) and so search out a basic degree of mutual social acceptability.

Often, of course, the changes needed are obvious and even comparatively easy to achieve. If, for example, when two people meet, 'both talk all the time, if both shout orders or ask questions ... there cannot be said to be social interaction at all.' But, 'between such extreme cases, and a well conducted interview or conversation between friends, there are degrees of co-ordination of techniques' (Argyle, 1967). These may concern *how much* speech occurs as well as *what* is being communicated; the *speed* of these verbal contributions; and *the accompanying physical and non-verbal pre-*

sentation of self, such as bodily posture and positioning, facial expression and frequency of eye contact.

However, other subtle but more influential features of this initial interaction may affect a group's evolving social organisation. Argyle, for example, suggests that, when relationships are being initiated, key issues to be settled include:

The degree of dominance to be permitted to different individuals —who speaks or acts most, or who defers most to others' contributions.

The levels of intimacy to be created—how close to each other individuals will sit or stand, how often they will touch each other and where, how often the eye gaze will be held and for how long, as well presumably as how personally revealing the content of verbal exchange will be.

The balance of competition and co-operation to be established.

The kind of 'emotional tone' to be generated—elation, boredom, anxiety, commitment, alienation.

These by themselves present difficult problems to would-be group members. But beyond them, even more basic questions may need answering. What, for example, are the boundaries of the group? Who, group members might wonder, is really *in* this group—who is here now but will not return a second time; who is absent today but intending to join next time; and which of the regular attenders are anyway *in* the group but yet not *of* it—that is, different in crucial respects from 'me and the others'. (The worker in particular may fall into this latter category and so may never be regarded as within the group's boundaries.)

Boundaries also have spatial and time dimensions. They are symbolised, for example, by how long and how often the group meets, by whether the group will always meet in the same place and by whether any future meeting place or times will be more or less confining. Until group members are clear about how the human, temporal and physical territory on which they are operating is to be circumscribed, they are bound to feel somewhat lost, and so, tentative in their commitment.

And beyond all this may be uncertainty about goals. Each group member will have his own reasons for joining the group, or at least for agreeing to attend on this occasion. However, little if any congruence may exist between these individual goals. Indeed, the values underlying them—what is thought of as good and bad and right and wrong—may be at variance, so that moves towards synchronisation on very basic issues may be needed. Individual differences may at this stage be so deep, leading to such sharp conflicts and strains, that synchronisation might even be unattainable. Even when the divisions are not this fundamental, a number of ill-fitting pieces will have to interlock, if a group structure, formal or informal, is to be established.

Usually, however, the emerging collectivity does not lack materials with which to build. No group is ever totally sealed off from the world outside. Its members initially, and then continuously while they remain members, inject key ingredients into the group's structure—values, goals, standards (norms), expectations about their own and others' behaviour (roles). These may repeatedly need to be adjusted to what others bring in and inject, and these adjustments may contribute significantly to that dynamic process of generating 'a distinctive group culture'. Moreover, what is brought in may not always be as relevant to the new group situation as its bearer assumes. Nonetheless, such imports are likely to dominate the first-stage exchanges and, because of their lack of synchronisation, to produce the strained atmosphere and cautious moves which so often characterise them.

The girls had by now settled down, and were talking rather more freely, though almost everything they said was bolstered by a swear word of one kind or another. Jenny described in some detail what good times she had at home on Friday and Saturday nights: 'I used to be out till after midnight many a time.' Ellen replied: 'I'd sometimes not get home till nearer two'—a statement which the others accepted without comment. I asked how their parents reacted when they stayed out so late, but Judy merely continued: 'Sometimes I'd get through five quid in a night on drink. And that's not counting what I had bought for me by lads.' Then Maggie suddenly looked straight at me and asked: 'Do you drink, Miss?' There was a little silence, as everyone looked at me, too, waiting for my answer (Community Home Girls' Group).

When I arrived at the camp with Tim, Pete and John, Miss R and Mr K were already there with two boys (Gary and Mark). Mr J turned up a few minutes later with Phil and Harry. The boys had met each other once before, for an hour or so in my office. For the first couple of hours, we unloaded food and equipment and packed it into the huts, made a meal and talked about what to do in the afternoon. The boys kept close together in their original groups, laughing more easily, it seemed, at each others' jokes than at ones coming from another sub-group. After lunch, they were let off the leash and began dashing around madly outside, climbing trees, daring each other to jump over the stream, throwing stones at the gatepost and generally going quite wild. The staff had to intervene a number of times, to calm them, to protect property, etc., but they invariably found something else to do to test us and each other. We finally decided we had better organise a trip out of some sort, as the only way to bring some order to the situation (Boys' Camp Group).

2. *Exploitive, instrumentally-focused exchanges* Striving for synchronisation assumes, of course, that something of an exchange process will get under way, often involving some (usually implicit) bargaining among the participating individuals. However, some individuals may well possess knowledge, skills or ideas which initially seem to them or to other group members to be specially relevant to the work of the group. They therefore are likely to have greatest power in the exchanges then beginning, and so may well strike bargains which are particularly advantageous to them.

These attempts by some participants to impart to others *their* view of what the group's aims, social structure and tasks should be may give this stage of a group's development two distinctive characteristics. It may mean, first, that many of the exchanges which occur are strikingly *egocentric* and so *exploitive*, one individual of another. And second, it may produce a group focus which is highly *instrumental*—that is, focused on those operations (pursuing activities in the out-of-doors, discussing relations with parents or boy-friends, planning a campaign against local housing department policies) which are instrumental in moving the group towards its overt and formal goals. There may be no intention among most group members to achieve individual gains via the group's ascribed tasks at the expense of any other individual group member. Nor will this necessarily be regarded as particularly desirable. Yet individual anxieties to get *some* form of group organisation established may be overwhelming and their effect very striking.

And so, provided they promise to bring some coherent purpose out of disorientation, and some orderly interaction out of chaos, norms can easily emerge which permit group members to inflict hurt or loss of face on each other. Indeed, at this stage, such behaviour may even in some groups be accepted as desirable (valuable) and encouraged at least as a tactical end.

Though they had now been considering the wording of the petition for over an hour, they still hadn't got beyond the first sentence. As the talking continued, I noticed Mrs Hallam had gone very quiet and was writing something on her own at the end of the table. Quite suddenly, she pushed the paper towards Mr Henry and said: 'How's that?' He glanced at it while Mr Raymond was speaking, said something like, 'Too wordy' and put it to one side. Mrs Baker asked what it was but Mr Henry more or less ignored her and responded to Mr Raymond's last comments. Mrs Hallam looked furious but said nothing until, much later, I, too, asked to see what she had written (Community Action Group).

This, it should be noted, is not necessarily how an outsider might appraise the group's development. If it were, the group might then be said to be dealing most effectively and confidently with its set tasks, or to be establishing an increasingly strong and appropriate form of social organisation. Rather, the labels 'egocentric' and 'exploitive' are being attached here in order to indicate how the interaction is often experienced by those actually involved in it. Demonstrations of the relevant behaviour may be rare, or only indirect—the language of casual conversation ('he put the knife in', 'that hurt' and so on) or the content and direction of certain jokes, may be all that reveals what is going on. Nonetheless, in the *expressive* areas of the group's life—in those areas of group activity where individuals express what is within and personal to them—some of the most frequently played roles may include 'victim' to someone else's 'assailant', 'sufferer' to someone else's 'tormentor' or 'martyr' to someone else's 'persecutor'. The subjective sense of being used for group ends may at this stage be very strong in many, even all, group members.

Such a situation does, of course, create opportunities for other types of behaviour. Less exploitive roles may be taken on— protector, healer, the drawer of hostile fire. Moreover, because many individuals do not *intend* to exploit, but think of themselves simply as focusing on the group's instrumental task, a strong base may be establishing itself for more individually affirmative responses in the future. Thus, though the way they play the roles may be hurtful, some group members may be beginning to try on such group-related roles as questioner, stimulator and interpreter (see Ruddock, 1969, Chapter 2).

Nonetheless, the price of an unwaveringly instrumental focus on a group's ascribed tasks can at this early stage, be very high. After all, other, much more expressive concerns, touching individuals' needs to synchronise their own private feelings and expectations, philosophies and social techniques, may, as we have already seen, rate a very high priority among group members. And so, individuals may be so 'used' within the group, that they leave it altogether. And others may invest a great deal, emotionally and intellectually, in roles which for social work purposes are unhelpful. Working hard on instrumental tasks may be crucial initially in giving group members common experiences and so in bringing them together more quickly and intimately. However, an overwhelmingly instrumental emphasis may in practice mean that important expressive tasks are avoided, and may give free rein to the exploitive exchanges to which, in any case, human interaction is prone in its early stages.

The effects of this type of interaction on the group's emerging social organisation can be far-reaching. Group boundaries may be drawn very tightly so that, for example, authority figures in particular, but also other participants, may be challenged to declare whether they are 'really' members of the group. These boundaries may also be staunchly defended and rigidly maintained : new members may not be welcome, and, in a two- or multi-group situation, the other group(s) may be perceived as radically different, as inferior, even as hostile.

And yet, despite such apparent external threats, internal morale —individual group members' shared feelings about their collective activities and organisation—may be low. The pain and personal rejection which many are experiencing will inevitably make them suspicious and frustrated. They are liable to become sceptical about, even alienated from, the group's activities. As a result, cohesion— that capacity to act together to achieve shared goals—may also be poor or fitful. Sub-groups may appear and may often be in conflict on issues unrelated to the group's stated purposes. Individuals may bid competitively for leadership, to the point where winning tactical skirmishes overrides all other considerations. Views of fellow group members and of the world outside may be so self-centred that working relations within the group become extremely unreliable.

3. *Affirmative, expressively-focused exchanges* Developments of this sort within a group almost certainly mean that the group's organisation no longer depends solely on what individuals originally imported into the group. Nor is it just the product of what has been imparted by group members, one to another. Rather, the importing and the imparting processes must involve, not simple, finite, one-way events, but *transactions*. What apparently takes place is an exchange—of attitudes, feelings, knowledge and services between two or more people, which generates more social and emotional capital than was originally invested. Traders from different cultures may never intend initially to do more than exchange goods. Repeatedly, however, they seem to intermarry and take on

some, at least, of each other's customs and ideas until ultimately they produce a culture with a new distinctiveness.

Something similar may occur during the development of a group's social organisation. Some values, goals, norms and even roles are clearly imported, and then imparted, from one group member to another. In the course of these transactions, however, new and unforeseen processes seem often to be set in motion. The transactions, in fact, will often generate values, goals, norms and so on which cannot be tracked back by simple progression to what any one individual has imported or merely imparted. They are the products of these particular individuals' experience of, and with, each other, of their interactions, in this situation. Individuals adjust, and are adjusted by, other individuals until they are adhering to elements of a social structure which differ to a greater or lesser degree from those which had their adherence in the first moments of the group's life.

Some of these self-generated features of group life can become extremely influential. Indeed, like the informal elements of group structure to which they may be closely related, they may even override what was originally imported into, and imparted within, the group. Thus, the tolerance—even positive endorsement—of emotional self-revelation as an acceptable way of behaving in the Community Home Girls' Group (p. 37) contrasted sharply with the norm of self-protection and self-aggrandisement as demonstrated in the group's very first meeting (p. 74). And similarly—though much less constructively from a social worker's point of view—the roles adopted by Phil and Mark quite later in their camp group experience (p. 63) were clearly creations of that particular experience and can hardly be said to have existed in that precise form when the group first came together (p. 74).

This, of course, is by no means inevitable. Nor is it necessarily 'good' by social work standards, since the exchanges may continue to be experienced by group members as exploitive. However, this phase of group life can, perhaps with social work help, gradually come to feel more supportive, encouraging and affirmative to the individuals most directly involved.

Again, a key question may be whether the group has begun to adjust its focus on instrumental tasks to its need to work also on expressive and synchronisation activities. For this adjustment to occur, norms will have to be established and reinforced which encourage or even require less egocentric actions from individuals. More positively, such norms in social work groups will probably need to stress a significant degree of other-directed behaviour. In some groups, in fact, such norms may even have to become positive values. Certain types of behaviour may then come to be regarded as good in themselves and not merely as means of attaining other, more long-term purposes, or purposes concerned more with things than with people. Showing concern and consideration for fellow group members, listening to what they say, or distributing satis-fying roles more equally, may thus come to be seen by the group as desirable in their own right, and not just because in the long run they enable the group to develop an impressive improvisation, con-duct a more orderly discussion or organise a successful petition.

In turn, such a regulation of group behaviour assumes certain dominant and rewarded roles in the group which contrast with those which predominated at an earlier stage of development. These may often focus on group maintenance, and so on the expressive rather than the purely instrumental tasks with which the group is continuously faced. As a result, individuals may be sought and encouraged who can act as collaborator, helper, go-between, en-courager. More specifically, the group may also need a signposter, or a recorder and/or recaller, or a teacher and resource person, or comforter, or a co-ordinator. Openings are likely to be created in fact for anyone who can contribute constructively to the group's collective as well as its separate, individual needs, and who can help it attain instrumental ends without undermining the social synchronisation which it may have striven so hard to establish. Developments in, for example, the Day Treatment Centre described by the officers illustrate this—like Fred's attempt to teach Arnie to read, Arnie's attempt to teach one of the POs to play crib-bage, and Bill's support for Alf and for Reg when they needed to press the DHSS for more money.

Indeed, at this stage, one of the more acceptable roles within a group may simply be that of 'person'. In other words, the group may have attained a tolerance of individual difference which allows it positively to encourage such differences, and to incorporate these without undue strain within its longer-term collective endeavours. Some of the emerging attitudes to Mrs Williams in the Wives' Group (p. 41) and to Jamie and Alf in the Day Treatment Centre (pp. 39 and 52) perhaps indicate this type of development, while the relative scarcity of such attitudes may help to explain some of the events in the Physically Handicapped Adolescent Group (p. 36) and in the Community Action Group (p. 75).

It can perhaps be seen from such examples that some of the main tasks of a group at this stage may be primarily with matters internal to the life and organisation of the group, e.g. distributing influence, rewards and status among group members in such a way as to enable all members to achieve greater satisfaction from

79

their group experience. Such reciprocity, in place of the earlier egocentricity, may produce a higher morale and cohesion, and may make the group's boundaries more flexible and so more responsive to newcomers and to outside influences. And, despite the apparent shift of emphasis away from specifically instrumental operations, it may also make the actual camping, discussion, or pressure-group campaigning far more effective.

Described in this way, a group at such a point in its evolution can easily seem to have reached the millennium. In reality, of course, perfect harmony is never attained, even assuming that it were desirable. Here, above all, the categorisation being outlined can be seen for what it is: a hypothetical model, which may help in the analysis of actual experience, but which can never claim to be a photographic representation of that experience. Sometimes, the line between individually exploitive and affirmative group experiences may be very sharp. Often, it will be vague and shifting. The mere conception of it, the mere fact that it may be said to exist and be sought out, may, however, sometimes deepen understanding of group behaviour very considerably and illuminate some of the meanings of human interaction, not least for those involved in it.

4. *Termination*   'Set-piece' groups in social work, however, no matter how harmonious they become, are never ends in themselves. Sooner or later, the main expressive task of the group may be neither synchronisation nor maintenance, but termination. In some groups (like, perhaps, the Community Action Group) this may never be the case, at least formally. In others (like the Wives' Club, perhaps) it may be a virtually permanent feature, as established contributors to the group's social organisation leave, to be replaced by others. In this case, termination and renewed synchronisation may be so closely enmeshed that neither is experienced by group members as an identifiable event or process.

In many groups in which social workers participate, however, termination is a very distinct experience. In part, this will mean that the instrumental tasks have to be wound up: the camp ended, the discussion stopped, the improvised drama presented in public, perhaps, and the group disbanded at the end of a school year.

However, just as earlier the expressive tasks which were concerned with achieving interpersonal synchronisation or overcoming egocentric exchanges absorbed considerable energy and feeling, so termination will also have very real social and emotional repercussions. Identification with what the group is doing, and with individuals who are known only as group members, may weaken. Indeed, some members may become very impatient that the group is carrying on at all. They may then claim that it should have been wound up even earlier, even though *any* termination date would probably have been preceded by a similar sense of disengagement.

Moves may also be made to re-establish or reinforce contacts which exist outside the group and which have nothing to do with it. Group members who do associate in non-group situations—women who are neighbours, boys who came to camp as friends—may be found, perhaps for the first time for months, actively relating again within the group. References may become more frequent to contacts and commitments outside the group—in the family, in friendship groups, at work or at school.

Group members may also try to clarify what they have gained from their group experience—to be sure that, after investing so much in the group's transactions, there really are dividends to be drawn. They may even try to embody these in some concrete form—in talisman-like gifts, signatures, badges and the rest. A ritual ending process—speeches, parties, formal presentations—may be instigated, and gestures made to continue the association, at least periodically. Some of the most striking and meaningful symbols of the group's shared experiences—its distinctive jargon, the events which make up its very own collection of myths and legends and amusing anecdotes, the special procedures it has adopted when getting certain things done—may all suddenly be treated rather lightheartedly, as if group members have begun to distance themselves from these facts of group life to some degree. The focus may shift repeatedly from looking back nostalgically, and even in ways tinged with mourning, to looking forward optimistically and expectantly, and then to looking backward again.

All this undoubtedly puts a premium on certain roles. To negotiate its termination adequately in an expressive as well as an instrumental sense, the group may at times need a historian, a paymaster capable of distributing the final rewards fairly and efficiently, and also a prophet capable of anticipating what lies in store in the next (outside) world. Also needed will be those who can reassure and support and, once again, protect the uncertain and the weak; who can interpret what is going on, and who can bring some order to events and changes once again threatening the group's existence.

For, increasingly, goals may again be becoming individualised, and some group members may be bewildered by the loss of the group's hard-won focus on the needs of others and of the group as a whole. Behaviour, therefore, which enables group members to make the transition to a future without the group, becomes permissible, and even especially desirable, though it may be now much less exploitive of others than it was at an earlier stage. So, too, is behaviour which actually weakens the group's boundaries and enables individuals to cross beyond them—which brings in outsiders, which links internal with external procedures and events, which increases awareness and understanding of what is peculiar to the group and what is normal outside it. If an affirmative, expressively sensitive phase has ever been experienced, these final developments may seem to group members to be proper, even inevitable, though still at times painful. If they have not, they may be felt to be unsatisfactory, a let down, since so much has been left undone, unfinished.

The emotional content of group interaction

No claim is made, of course, that this artificial ordering of a complex reality is objective or value-free. In the context of social work practice, 'good' and 'bad' ways of organising group transactions must be acknowledged, whether the vantage point is that of the worker or the client. That is why terms like 'exploitive' and 'affirmative' have been used unashamedly, and why certain phases of group development have been described as more 'helpful' to group members' needs than others.

Nor, of course, does the scheme imply that individuals' experiences in groups are emotion-free, and that the whole process of group development is merely a mechanical one. For convenience' sake, terms like 'organisation', 'structure' and 'component elements' have been used. Nonetheless, the individuals who become group members continue to feel, and respond repeatedly, on the basis of these feelings. It is they, and not just an omniscient and manipulating outsider, who decide which values, goals, norms, roles, statuses and so on will become significant and which will not. They do so on many irrational as well as rational grounds, which are very often, of course, quite outside the control or even influence of some intervening worker. And, having done so, they feed responses, pressures, choices and much else back into the interactional process of the group, which, in turn, go far to determine how the interaction will evolve.

Indeed, the affective dimensions of group life are much more complex even than this transactional model would suggest. For the emotional content of human exchanges can be understood only as a recurring series of ambivalences. Initially, for example, individuals may join a group feeling apprehensive, resentful or suspicious. And yet at the same time they may be hopeful (if only secretly) that they will enjoy and gain from it, or (again perhaps secretly) even *expect* some benefits, and so be susceptible to its influences.

Or again, individuals may come full of self-doubt, comparing themselves unfavourably with other group members. And yet, they may be pleased they have been invited; or reassured that they have overcome the first hurdle of actually coming at all; and/or they may be scornful of all the other people (including the worker) who need to join such a group, and feel themselves to be there only under duress or by accident.

Such ambivalences are, of course, entirely normal in human beings. They are therefore likely to exist within all group members to some degree, and to interfere—in the exact, 'radio' sense of the word—with verbal and non-verbal communication and reception within the group. Thus, what is said may not be properly heard, what is done not accurately observed, so that the meaning of the communicator is received in an incomplete or distorted form. On the other hand, the tensions set up by individuals' ambivalences—their need at least partially to resolve the conflicting emotions—can powerfully motivate them, especially where the 'positive' and 'helpful' emotions can be identified and tapped.

Yet these ambivalences can never be completely eradicated. At an exploitive-instrumental stage of a group's development, an individual may feel simultaneously elated that he has begun to find a role and status for himself and yet guilty about how he is achieving these. Or, at an affirmative-expressive stage, he may enjoy a sense of trust and intimacy within the group, and yet be anxious that he is revealing too much of himself or, again, guilty, that he *is* enjoying such self-indulgence. And, when termination comes, he may simultaneously experience regret at what he is losing, and pleasure that he cannot use elsewhere what he has acquired in this group.

Finally, though such ambivalent feelings are clearly internal and often private reactions within each individual group member, they can be seen as supporting once again the interactionist perspective on which this chapter has relied. For they suggest that what is publicly seen of an individual within a group situation is not necessarily the only 'him' or 'her' which exists. Rather, the public presentation of the self in the group may simply be the outcome of the individual selecting, for *these* circumstances and for *this* moment, from a wide range of possible behaviours that which seems most appropriate. The unchosen alternatives could theoretically have expressed a great many other private and often conflicting feelings he is then experiencing, and would therefore have produced some very different public versions of the same 'self' (see especially Goffman, 1959).

6

Group tasks and their impact

A group and its tasks

The emphasis of the last chapter was on how the people who join a group affect each other and organise their relationships. And yet, inseparable from the interactional dimensions of group experience are those aspects of that experience which are concerned with what the group actually does. For, all groups carry on some form of activity—they 'work' at something, they undertake some sort of instrumental operations in order to achieve their individual or collective ends. Through these 'tasks', it is possible for the social worker to be extremely helpful to his clients.

The practical meaning of the term 'task' can, as we have seen, vary considerably. Certainly 'work' in this context does not only mean 'labour' but can also include 'play' and 'recreation'. Also, 'task' may involve something highly organised and having a clear-cut, even a concrete and measurable, outcome. Alternatively, it may be diffuse in its organisation and leave no tangible evidence of what has resulted. Thus, on the one hand, some groups sit in a circle, discuss quite specific issues and reach definite conclusions; or they climb to the top of mountains; or they petition and write pamphlets and hold public meetings until they have changed a council's housing policies. On the other hand, other groups 'merely' fool about on street corners, or drink beer and joke in a pub, or natter over cups of tea. In some groups, of course, both types of work occur simultaneously. All, however, are active on the specific activities essential to attaining their particular goals.

Given this broad conception of activity, it is difficult to imagine a group in which no activity occurs. In fact, despite all that was said in the last chapter about the human dimensions of group experience, it is the *activity* of a group with which most people— and certainly most uninvolved outsiders—are usually preoccupied.

Thus, a group is often judged by outsiders—indeed, its very existence is often justified—solely by what it does and how well it does it. What did the group talk about, the critic asks: was the discussion logical and thoughtful, or did it flounder? Or, Which route did the group take up the mountain and did everyone manage to get to the top? or, How many people signed the petition, and how relevant were the speeches at the public meeting? A group which is found wanting on these counts is always in danger of being judged 'bad' or a 'failure'.

What happens in a group is not assessed only by outsiders, however. The people who are actually members of that group will also have a point of view, and *their* criteria for judging the group may be very different. In the first place, as we saw in the last chapter, a group is a setting in which individuals express a great many current, rational and emotional, expectations, perceptions and evaluations. And these apply, not just to what is done, but also to other individuals and their relations with them. Indeed, such expressive behaviour may not only be irrelevant to the group's formal tasks: it may even be intended (though not always consciously, of course) to damage or block work on those tasks. The value of the group to those taking part may thus have little or nothing to do with what the group is ostensibly formed to do—that is, the discussion, mountain-climbing, petitioning and so on. Once again, an 'internal' frame of reference may have to be adopted.

However, even when an individual does care about discussion, or climbing mountains, or pressuring the powers-that-be on housing policies, what he regards as worthwhile in such activity may not be what the outsider would assume, or even what other participants judge as worthwhile for them. For, though the activity may be undertaken collectively, what is derived from it will, as we have seen, ultimately be highly individual. The gain for each participant will be received and felt by them in a very personal, even private way, and so may differ substantially from any other individual's gains.

The implication of all this is therefore twofold. First, the *meaning* of a group's experience and activity may again be one thing for the onlooker and outside judge, and quite another for the actual participant.

The meeting finally ended just after 11, with everyone apparently talked-out and exhausted. I went down the stairs with Mrs Baker and Mr Raymond, and stood chatting in the street with them for a few moments about the progress made. Mrs Baker in particular seemed despondent, despite what had been achieved. As we parted she remarked, almost in passing and to herself: 'Well, we did give Stan Henry a good run for his money, anyway!' (Community Action Group)

We finished the improvisation for the second time on the (second) afternoon and sat together on benches and on the floor recovering. Most of the group were clearly waiting for me to make the next move, and eventually I understood why. For, after a few moments of hesitation, Debbie suddenly asked: 'Have you found out enough about us now to tell the Head?' (Physically Handicapped Adolescent Group).

And second, the meaning of a group's experience and activity may be one thing for one participant, something else for a second participant, something else for a third, and so on, according to however many group members there are.

We sat and ate our sandwiches at the top. The boys sheltered behind a rock from the strong wind just out of my sight, while I tried to boil up some water for a brew and Mr K pored over the map a little way away, trying to work out the best route down. The view of the valley and the lake was magnificent and crystal clear. As they ate, the boys began to discuss the climb. 'Bloody stupid,' Phil was saying. 'What do they want to drag us all the way up here for? Just to show us how bleedin' good they are?' Peter replied: 'I dunno, I enjoyed it. Getting to the top was really good.' 'At least we showed 'em we could do it, after all the names they've called us this week,' Gary added. But neither Phil nor Harry were convinced. Phil remarked: 'Who cares what they bleedin' well think.' 'Anyway,' John concluded, 'I like it up here. I never done anything like this before. I never been so high I could see everything spread out like that.' Phil's only comment was: 'Fuck!' (Boys' Camp Group).

Social work criteria for evaluating group activity

And yet, though generalised and external judgments about the value of a group's activity are risky and inevitably partial, social workers will frequently have to make such judgments. Indeed, much of this chapter is written on the assumption that a social worker may at times need some special understanding of what an activity might do to or for clients, and some extra opportunities to influence that activity's development. Repeatedly, there will be the implication that the worker might modify what is done within a group already established and pursuing its self-selected tasks (say, a teenage 'gang' or a community self-help committee); or that he might introduce activities not yet considered by such a group. Alternatively, in a group which the worker himself is initiating, it is often implied that he select the key activities himself, or influence their selection, and that he do so according to *his* perceptions of the impact they might have on participants.

The extent to which a worker can or should assume his special wisdom and power will of course vary. In some circumstances, his manipulating and/or imposition will be justified: how else, for example, would a number of isolated individuals with a common problem (like unsupported mothers or physically handicapped teenagers) ever get to talk or do things together, if social workers did not sometimes deliberately try to bring them into contact in the first place? In other circumstances, the worker may not be able to claim either the right or the need to be as directive as this, as much experience with community action groups and spontaneous recreational groups demonstrates.

Whatever the precise circumstances, however, the need for a more deliberate analysis of group activities would seem, in social work no less than in many other 'helping' professions, to be long overdue. For, decisions about what a social work group should do, and evaluations of what it has done, seem repeatedly to rely on untested, and often highly subjective, assumptions. In particular, the 'goodness' or worth of an activity (whether positive or negative) seems repeatedly to be taken, without question or criticism, to be intrinsic to that activity. That is, the activity is judged to be, *by its very nature*, 'character-building', or 'cathartic', or inherently capable of developing 'responsible attitudes to the community'. Or, alternatively, it is dismissed as 'pointless' 'worthless' or as having no 'cultural value'. Decisions about what are valuable collective tasks thus, time and again, seem to stem primarily from the (often unspoken and unsupported) ideological beliefs of a sponsoring agency or of a particular worker, rather than from any careful examination of what *really* happens to the individuals who take part in the activities concerned.

What is more, even these highly subjective statements often seem to be aimed mainly at justifying what an organisation or a worker needs and prefers to do for *their own* comfort and confidence, and rather less at ensuring the selection of activities particularly appropriate to the group and its individual members. True, much theorising takes place, especially in the context of casework, about 'diagnosing' clients' special needs and then 'prescribing' appropriate 'treatment' (that is, helpful forms of joint worker-client activity). And, though the limitations of this kind of individualised

87

approach are, as we saw in Chapter 1 very real, such statements may indeed represent what actually happens, at least in casework.

However, in group work, such attempts at careful matching of individual needs with group activity seem far less frequent or self-conscious. Some very generalised statements may be made about the appropriateness of a certain activity to a certain type of person. Some people may be seen as too young or too old for one form of activity. Others may be included or ruled out because they are male or female. A third group may be judged on the basis of such personal characteristics as speech defects or broken legs. On the whole, however, the underlying if largely unspoken assumption seems to be that many broad categories of client will inevitably benefit from the performance of a particular task. Its value for individuals, it seems, is therefore virtually absolute and universal.

What is more, certain broadly defined tasks—notably 'discussion', 'outdoor pursuits' and 'community service'—have over the years accrued very special credit among social workers, so that today they are widely, and often uncritically, used in group situations. The reasons for their pre-eminence are not difficult to find. Thus, discussion—verbal exchanges between worker and client—has been the main, even the only, form of joint activity in which many social workers seem to have felt at all comfortable. A major extension of it from casework to group work was therefore almost inevitable. Group work is thus now frequently seen, not so much as social work carried on by another means, but as casework carried on in a somewhat modified form in a rather different setting. Verbal exchanges with clients conducted one at a time are thereby replaced by verbal exchanges carried on with a number of clients simultaneously. It may save time; it may even make the casework more effective; and it is certainly worth trying when the one-to-one verbal exchanges reach an impasse. In any case, all around there are probably others 'giving it a try', which in itself exerts a pressure to become involved.

The resort to outdoor pursuits would often seem to result from similar motives. Again, there may be some practical need to find a more productive alternative to casework. And there may also be the temptation to settle for something which is fashionable and, for many social workers, familiar. Certainly, many adults working within the helping services seem to have derived a great deal of personal satisfaction from outdoor activities and to have come to feel comfortable with them. In a somewhat arbitrary and intuitive way, they have apparently, then, turned a private, recreational interest into a professional method. Add the well-advertised (and well-financed) conviction among many educationalists and industrialists that outdoor pursuits have an intrinsic capacity for building 'character', and it is hardly surprising that they have been widely adopted as a group activity with clients.

Community service is a rather later addition to the social worker's repertoire of group activities, and has apparently been accepted by them reluctantly. Indeed, it has often had to be imposed from outside as a consequence of the development of intermediate treatment, and of such legislation as the Criminal Justices Act, 1972. Motives here seem more mixed and complex. Some influential sections of our society apparently see service to one's community as one, at least indirect, way of getting criminals and other deviants to repay something to those they have harmed. Alternatively, or additionally, such 'treatment' may be looked on as a necessary and cheap way of supplementing public and welfare services which are overburdened and under-financed. There is also, it seems, a widespread belief that doing good to others is good for the doer—that it can change socially undesirable attitudes and behaviour and give individuals a new sense of themselves and their place in society. Again, therefore—even though in this case social workers may not be fully convinced—it seems to be widely assumed that benefits for clients are inevitably embodied within the very activity of community service.

Other forms of group activity are of course used by social workers. Wives and mothers sew and cook together, children paint and build and climb in playgroups, adolescents play football or table-tennis or visit the seaside. And in some cases, the activity is indeed inherently justified, in that its product—such as the dresses or the children's clothes sewn by the mothers—are of enormous practical use to the participants or their families.

Nonetheless, the criteria for choosing or endorsing an activity seem, in a large number of cases, to be highly intuitive and/or ideological. The workers concerned, and often (even if less consciously) the clients too, undoubtedly hope for gains which they can experience socially and emotionally. And yet they frequently appear to lack reliable guidelines for seeking out and measuring such gains.

What do activities do to people?

If social workers were prepared to give it sufficient priority, however, there is now no doubt that they could attempt a much more sophisticated analysis and appreciation of the activities they use in their group work programmes. Some of the earliest efforts in this field were concerned with children's games, and were carried out in the United States. Nonetheless, they have implications for all forms of small-group activity everywhere.

Gump and Sutton-Smith (1955) began in the 1950s to examine what they called the 'It' role in children's games. These are the games in which one child who is chosen to be 'on' becomes the central person, the focus of the interest, responses, and feelings for all the other participants. What in effect Gump and Sutton-Smith asked was: How do the expectations and perceptions attached to an 'It' role affect the individual playing it, and also the other participants? How far does the performance of the role vary, not only according to the personality of the individual occupying it, but also according to the particular version of the game being played and the special demands made by the role as it is defined in that particular game? In other words, how far are individual 'meanings' which are attached to the role influenced—perhaps even controlled —by the 'game-given' elements of the role?

Gump and Sutton-Smith's observations and research (Gump and Sutton-Smith, 1955; Sutton-Smith, 1955) suggested answers to these questions which, for social workers, seem highly significant. For example, they showed how the *power* in the 'It' role can vary very considerably from game to game, and that it may be important for a social worker to take such differences into account when planning his group work. Thus, the person who is 'on' in Simon Says can control almost all the actions of all the other players. In Blind Man's Buff, on the other hand, the central person is largely at the mercy of the other players, to the extent that making a fool of him or her is virtually an integral part of the game.

Moreover, the degrees of power in the 'It' role do not vary only according to which *type* of game is played. They vary also within the same general category of game, depending on which form of that game is chosen. As Sutton-Smith (1955, p. 262) points out:

> In Simple Tag, 'It' has to pursue the other players, chasing whichever players he wishes. But in the game of Cross Tag, if any running player passes between 'It' and the player he is chasing at that moment, then the 'It' must chase this new player who has crossed in front of him. This means then in the game of Cross Tag the 'It' is being confronted continually with fresh players. In consequence, in Cross Tag, the 'It' has much less power than in Simple Tag.

To the social worker who has never contemplated organising games sessions for children, all this may seem rather academic. However, it does suggest at least one vital general conclusion: that, regardless of whether an activity has certain built-in *qualities* and *values*, it may—indeed, almost certainly will—have certain *significant*, *controlling* effects on how participants behave. Thus, the precise impact of an activity—discussion, rock-climbing, petitioning or whatever—cannot be said to be determined only by who takes part. It may depend at least as much on what the activity does to these participants—on the demands and limitations which its essential structure imposes on them. Almost inevitably, in fact, an activity seems to *coerce* the behaviour of group members, at least to some extent.

Sutton-Smith (1951, p. 263) illustrates the practical implications of this analysis very vividly:

> The boy is Freddy, nine years old, moderately skilled in games, but distrustful, withdrawn and unpopular. The first game is Tail Snatch—a game in which the 'It' person stands facing the backs of the rest of the group, all of whom wear loosely tied tails. 'It', calls a series of signals.... [on the final one] 'It' races towards the rest of the group and they flee towards a safety area. 'It' tries to collect as many tails as he can.... At first Freddy refused to play the game; later he was persuaded to play. In the 'It' role, he was at first reluctant and uncertain; then he experienced moderate success. With each capture of a tail, his stance was more confident, his chasing more vigorous; finally as his tension melted away, he began to laugh.... The game ingredient which contributed to Freddy's pleasurable experience was that of a Central Person role which had considerable *game-given power*—'It' had the initiative and could surprise; *'It' was free of game retaliation*. This 'It' role required only a *moderate amount of physical competence*—an amount which Freddy possessed.
>
> In the second game, a Cat attempts to catch a Mouse. A circled group joins hands and attempts to block the cat and protect the mouse. Freddy becomes the cat and is initially excited and assertive. But he has no success. The mouse continually taunts him; the group has him 'on the spot' and is obviously enjoying it. Freddy blusters that he will use a 'special trick'—but the trick doesn't work. Freddy scowls, sticks out his tongue at the mouse. After several more hopeless attempts to catch the mouse, Freddy, in a sullen temper, quits the game.

Freddy withdraws because he is in an 'It' role 'that lacks game-given power, and thus requires more ability and strength than Freddy has.'

Here, Gump and Sutton-Smith show how different types of 'It' role can coerce players' behaviour in very different ways. As a result, it seems likely that, as the same individual moves from one role to the other, the perceptions of, and feelings about himself and others which the individual takes away—that is, the 'lessons' he learns—may differ significantly as a result of the in-built, internal structure of the activity. If this is in fact so, then social workers will surely need to make this more deliberate analysis of group activities much more a part of their stock-in-trade.

The ingredients of group activity

It is not, of course, only the power of particular assigned roles which might be coercive within an activity. Potentially, activities might coerce a very wide *range* of individual behaviour and inter-action, even though the actual *extent* and *strength* of the coercion will vary from activity to activity. Gump and Sutton-Smith provide something of a check-list, which suggests that consideration might need to be given to such variables as:

the degree of skill required;
the degree of competitiveness stimulated;
the amount of bodily contact provoked or permitted;
the degree of interdependence stimulated among players;
the degree of leeway permitted for responses on impulse;
the rewards and penalties available, and how long these are delayed.

Given some reflection on these, and other, variables, it might (just) be possible for a social worker to consider in advance what the potential effects of an activity might be and whether they are likely to have helpful or unhelpful meanings for participants.

An attempt to build this check-list into a fuller and more practical framework has been made by another American, Robert Vinter (Vinter, 1967b). Vinter looks at what individuals do within an activity from two points of view: behaviour which is *essential* to performing the activity, and behaviour which arises out of performing the activity but which is more of a *personal response* to it. Examples of the first (which he calls *constituent behaviour*) might include:

Verbal exchanges in a discussion group
Walking and climbing during a mountain-climbing expedition
Drafting a statement for a petition, or making a speech in public

Examples of the second (or, as Vinter calls them, *respondent*) types of behaviour might include:

Offering cigarettes round at an especially tense moment of a
group discussion

Racing other individuals to the top of a rise during a fell-walking
expedition

Organising a 'social' for those actively involved in the pressure
group campaign

Constituent behaviour is thus another way of describing that behaviour which is coerced by the activity. Respondent behaviour,
on the other hand, sums up how individuals extemporise on, and
perhaps even break through, these coercive elements and to a
greater or lesser degree impose their own personal improvisations
and individual patterns on what is done.

Clearly, constituent (essential or coerced) behaviour and
respondent (non-essential or improvised) behaviour are very hard to
separate. And yet, some understanding of how they might emerge
within a specific activity, and of what the balance between them is,
could be of enormous use to a worker and his clients. Ways therefore need to be found of identifying those ingredients of an activity
which determine constituent behaviour, and which make respondent behaviour possible.

One of Vinter's main contributions to group work theory has
been to propose an initial framework for conducting just such an
analysis. Vinter points in particular to six main dimensions of
group life which significantly affect action and interaction within
a group:

1. How *prescriptive* a particular activity is—that is, how far the
activity does, by its very nature, lay down what participants may
do with the various parts of their body, how precisely they must
act, how freely they may improvise, and so on. Two 'discussion
groups' may illustrate the point:

> The girls arrived singly or in pairs, within 10 minutes of each
> other. Each took a chair in the small circle which the worker
> had set out beforehand, until all the chairs were filled. The
> girls remained seated for about 45 minutes, and contributed to
> the discussion with varying degrees of frequency and intensity.
> At one point, two of them exchanged cigarettes. Later, the
> worker got up to search on her desk for a paper. Eventually,
> she indicated that the session was over. Apart from one girl,
> they all got up from their chairs and left the room (Community
> Home Girls' Group).

> The mothers arrived singly and in pairs over a period of

about half-an-hour. Mrs Williams, the first arrival, immediately put the kettle on and began to set out the cups. Mrs Jones and Mrs Graham came in together and helped Mrs Williams by getting trays out of cupboards, pouring the boiling water into the tea-pot, refilling the kettle, and putting out ash-trays on the coffee tables. They, and Mrs Etchells then began to hand round cups of tea and biscuits, carrying sugar from table to table and talking briefly with people as they did so. After about 30 minutes, about ten women had arrived and three sub-groups, each carrying on a separate conversation, had formed in different parts of the room. Two groups were standing, one was sitting. After about an hour and a half, Mrs Harding left, and within the next half-an-hour, in twos and threes, she was followed by all the others (Wives' Club).

These situations are, of course, sketched out only in very simple terms. However, they do perhaps illustrate the basic differences between two groups whose 'core' activity might be given the same label—'discussion'—but whose organisation of that activity pre-scribes individuals' behaviour in very different ways. The Com-munity Home Girls' Group at the particular meeting described required that its members sit, face each other in a circle, remain in quite close physical proximity, not hide any part of their body behind tables, not normally move about the room, and arrive and depart at more or less fixed moments in time. In addition, two of the members had to place themselves immediately next to the authority figure in the group (the worker).

The Wives' Club, on the other hand, apparently prescribed seat-ing, movement, physical proximity, bodily presentation of oneself and the time dimensions of the exchanges far less exactly. It did coerce verbal exchanges, and may even have made them *more* essential than in the Community Home group. And it also required other types of social behaviour (such as tea-making, handing round cups and so on). However, even within these constituent be-haviours, a good deal of improvisation (respondent behaviour) was possible.

Of course, any group activity must prescribe individual behaviour and interaction to some extent. However, to understand this pre-scriptiveness and *how* it affects individual responses, it is necessary to do much more than simply describe the activity and give it a general title like 'discussion'. It is necessary also to ask such questions as: What procedures and rituals have to be followed? What type of bodily actions are called for? How many such actions are required? How important are these actions for the completion

of the activity? What other types of action are thereby automatically prevented? And a social worker then needs to add the no less
crucial question: How might *group members* answer these questions—that is, what meaning do they attach to such prescriptiveness?

2. Who or what *controls* individuals' behaviour and interaction
within an activity, and how extensive is this control? Every activity
thus has built into it certain prescriptions which, as long as the
individual continues to agree to take part, must limit what he or
she can and cannot do and how he or she may do it. These limitations, it should be noted, are not *directly* concerned with participants' *interaction*, though this may be severely affected by them.
They are focused above all on the actions which any individual
may undertake in direct relation to the task(s) in hand. Such
limitations may be overt or hidden, stringent or lax. In the end, an
individual may choose whether or not to accept them, though
if he refuses, the only course of action left open to him may be to
cease participating in the activity, and so perhaps to leave the
group. Nonetheless, however the limitations are expressed and
however they operate, they suggest that regulators—controls—on
individual behaviour, and therefore on individuals' interactions
with each other, must be present in any activity.

Some of these controls may be external to the actual activity and
unchangeable, while others may be internal to it and/or open to
change. Thus, in most sports and games, a key control is inevitably
the rules of play. These are usually so integral to what is done that
they cannot easily be manipulated by participants: part of the
contract each person enters into when joining the activity is that he
accepts the rules as given. In addition, there may also be individuals
—referees, umpires, judges, adjudicators—who do not participate
directly in the core tasks, but who interpret and enforce the rules.
They thus act as final, and powerful, arbiters over what goes on
and/or over how success is measured, and so are key regulators of
individual behaviour.

Individuals *within* an activity—the 'It' person, chairmen of committees, climbing instructors, discussion group leaders—may also
exercise this kind of control. They may even have the power to
decide who takes part and who does not, and for how long they
participate. In this case, however, the position and strength of the
control may be open to change. Sometimes this change may occur
quickly and often (as with many 'It' roles); sometimes only slowly
and rarely (as, for example, with most committee chairmen).

Internal controls over members' behaviour thus represent a vari-
able of some significance for social workers. They and/or their

clients can often manipulate it, doing so in ways which are either helpful or unhelpful to themselves and other clients. The two games described by Sutton-Smith (see p. 96 above) illustrate this clearly. In both games, the externally imposed rules act as an inescapable form of control. However, in the first game, Freddy, as 'It', exercises considerable control over the other players, in the second game, little if any such control. Indeed, in the second game, he is largely controlled by them. Both his own, and his playmates' behaviour and subsequent reactions inevitably change as the nature and position of this control alters.

Yet, though internal controls may be more amenable to change (by a worker or a client) than external controls, the latter are rarely completely unbendable. Sometimes, the rules of a game or sport can be modified to suit different participants. (The development of five-a-side football, in all its variations, is a good example of this.) Sometimes, too, participants can play the key controlling roles of referee or even judge. At the very least, precautions can be taken not to saddle a group with an activity whose controls (rules, referees, chairmen, 'It' roles, and so on) have such unpleasant or unhelpful 'meanings' for participants that the activity ends up producing a negative rather than a positive experience for them.

By the third day, the novelty of the work had certainly worn off. A great deal of woodwork had to be given two coats of paint, and this often called for considerable precision and concentration and showed results only very slowly. The wallpaper chosen by the warden of the hostel had a complicated pattern, so that Alf, as the only relatively experienced home decorator amongst us, had to take almost sole charge of the paper-hanging. This left Fred and Don underemployed for much of the time, so that they became very restless. And, to make matters worse, the warden was by now pressing us very hard to get the room finished for some special event he had on at the weekend, which meant that I had to be continually chivvying the men to keep at it. After lunch, I virtually had a mutiny on my hands, and had to adopt some quite strong-arm tactics to get them back to work (Day Treatment Centre).

3. *What kinds of bodily movement* does the activity allow and/ or require? Clearly, this question, like that about controls, significantly overlaps with the one concerned with the prescriptiveness of behaviour. However, in this case, the focus is not on the *range* of actions which the activity allows a participant, but on the *nature* and *form* of those actions. What a worker needs to be asking here

is not How many actions may a participant indulge in? and How free is he to choose whether or not to act in those ways? It is rather What precisely can he do with his body while carrying out those actions and what are the effects?

To these general questions, social workers seem again, often, to have some ready, very intuitive answers. It seems to be widely accepted, for example, that vigorous bodily movement can be very therapeutic—that, as physical energy is released, pent-up emotional and nervous energy will probably also find an outlet. And so, aggressively inclined adolescent boys are encouraged to play exhausting games of football, or to flog themselves to the tops of mountains; and 'acting-out' girls to dance frantically all evening.

Even these insights, however, might become a little more refined. For bodily movement is not simply a matter of how much ground the *whole* body covers, or how much energy *in total* is expended It also means considering how many parts of the body move, and how precise and controlled those movements are.

And so, a discussion group which normally requires the movement of only eye, tongue, lips and jaw, could (as the Wives' Club, p. 93 shows) be so arranged that, where relevant, far more physical mobility occurs. As a result, the verbal exchanges might flow much more freely. Or that general category of activity normally labelled 'drama' might produce a much wider and more expressive range of physical movement if, not just the role-play to which social workers seem most frequently to turn, but also versions of it which might be labelled 'improvisation' or 'dance drama' were sometimes introduced. The *individual* expressiveness of this type of bodily movement could be extremely helpful to many of those who become social work clients.

No less important may be the place of bodily movement in a group's *interaction* processes. Physical contact between people in our society—whether between man and man, woman and woman, or woman and man—is ruled by some very strict taboos. Whether these taboos are helpful or inhibiting will, of course, once again depend on the particular individuals concerned and their special needs. It may be extremely important, therefore, for social workers to consider the physical dimensions of a group's activities, and ask in particular what these activities do for group members' physical interactions. Do the activities encourage or discourage physical contact? If they encourage it, what type of contacts will result and in what circumstances? Will the contacts be mainly one-to-one, or will they simultaneously involve all, or most, group members? When, in the development of the activity, will these contacts occur? And what will they mean for participants?

The scene now changed to a hospital. Ray came staggering in, supported by Geoff, with Eric in close, hovering attendance. Ray was laid down on a 'bed', and Becky and Jenny acted as nurses. Becky was by now very excited and couldn't play out the role very easily, though she expressed some genuine affection towards Ray. But Jenny took the part extremely seriously, examining Ray's head, covering him over with a blanket, arranging his feet comfortably and so on. At this point, Debbie came in, playing the doctor. In her effort to be stern and important, she controlled her limp in a way I've never seen before. Her 'examination' of Ray included looking into his eyes very carefully, listening to his heart (she put her ear very close to his chest and kept tapping it with the knuckle of one finger!), holding his wrist to take his pulse, fingering his head 'wound' and tapping his knees (Debbie has obviously had plenty of 'full physicals' in her short life!).... The whole scene seemed to suggest new acceptance of each others' handicap, and also of each other's sex. Certainly, they showed a good deal less self-consciousness with each other this afternoon, and especially the boys with the girls, than they have in the past (Physically Handicapped Adolescent Group).

4. How much *skill* in the activity is needed, not to excel but merely to take part? Overall, this chapter is concerned with the 'work' which groups undertake—with the tasks and actions which are instrumental to their achieving often explicit and perhaps even concrete objectives. Mothers have to learn to cope with families on their own, and so 'work' at discussing the problems this produces and at actually providing company for each other; adolescents want to enjoy themselves, 'get away from it all', and cement friendships, and so they work at camping and at climbing a mountain; residents of a particular area want to prevent their houses being bull-dozed, and so they work at drawing up petitions, getting signatures for those petitions, and presenting them to local government officials.

Clearly, the degree of skill needed by these forms of work varies considerably. It will depend on exactly what the aim is, how determined individuals are to achieve it and how important high-level achievement is to them personally. The adolescents mentioned above, for example, will probably need a wider and more sophisticated range of techniques to scale a rock-face than to climb the mountain by marked paths as part of an afternoon's leisure stroll; just as the mothers may need a more highly developed degree of confidence to talk about their sexual difficulties while their husbands are 'away' than to discuss how to manage the family budget each week.

And so, to talk about skill in mountain-climbing or in discussion or in petitioning is to describe what is involved only in a very generalised and crude way, whether the aim is to do well or simply to take part. When 'mountain-climbing' means 'rock-climbing' it will almost certainly demand a range of skills, not all of which will be required for fell-walking. These skills may include a very precise use of the fingers and toes, as well as other, even more subtle forms of physical and emotional competence, such as a sharp use of the eyes, very refined bodily balance, judgment about when to move which part of the body how far, and a sense of one's own limit-ations. And it will also demand some social skills, since rock-climbers cannot normally operate safely and successfully on a face without being prepared to relate to other climbers whom they may or may not like personally.

When considering activities from the point of view of the skill required, the social worker thus cannot afford to rely totally on crude criteria like: Have these adolescents the physical stamina to climb?, or Can these mothers discuss? A rather more detailed analysis of the skills involved may be needed, so that clients' com-petence in some of the component elements of an activity can be considered. If the residents have never before even considered contradicting officials, they may not even be aware of the possibility of petitioning, still less of what precise techniques this calls for. If mothers, as children, were taught by experience as well as precept, to be seen and not heard, they may not be very practised at such basic discussion techniques as formulating ideas in words, or distinguishing fact from fantasy and from opinion, or even listen-ing carefully to what their adversary says. Even 'mountain-climbing', as we have seen, has a variety of meanings and involves a multitude of skills.

The first consideration about skill is, therefore, Exactly what does it mean in any particular activity? But a second, and no less impor-tant, question in the context of this book is: How much skill is needed *merely to take part* in any particular activity? The emphasis is crucial, but seems often to need special explanation. For, social workers no less than others, may consider competence largely as something which brings achievement. They may never deliberately consider it as something which simply permits participation. Yet, if an individual has this very basic competence, he can at least be involved with others and perhaps gain some personal acceptance and feedback, regardless of whether, in the 'work' of the group, he does well. Social workers frequently meet individuals who lack this acceptance in their lives and who, because of a history of personal failure in such 'work' areas, doubt their ability ever to succeed in them. For them, therefore, the criterion of *mere capacity to join in* would seem to be crucial.

> Because the boys weren't used to going to bed early at home, and there was 'nowhere to go' after dark, we had brought a number of simple games with us to fill the evening hours. One of these was Bingo, which seemed a good starter and which we assumed the boys would know all about through their parents' enthusiasm for the game. Gary got very restless as soon as we suggested it, and was soon irritating the others by his funny remarks and refusal to follow his own card carefully. Then Mark suddenly said: 'If *you* aren't quick enough to keep up, thick 'ead, the rest of us are. And I'd like that bar o' chocolate, so shut your gob.' It was only then that we realised how much difficulty Gary had in even understanding numbers and reading them off his card (Boys' Camp Group).

All this implies that, where the social worker is in a position properly to do so, he may need to consider very carefully whether the skills called for by a group's activity really do permit all group members to participate in—for them—a meaningful way. In addition, even after group members have embarked on an activity, or where the worker enters an established group like an adolescent peer group or an adult community action group, he may need to try to help group members to pitch the level of competence demanded at a point where general and satisfying participation is possible.

5. How much *interaction* among group members does the activity require or permit? The focus here is on the *exchange among participants* (verbal and non-verbal) which the activity, by its very nature, encourages or demands. Since it is *group* activity which we are discussing, this may seem to raise only obvious and indisputable issues; interaction is after all, as we saw in the last chapter, an essential ingredient of all such situations.

And yet, social workers' understanding of this too often lacks subtlety. For, the amount and nature of the interaction which any activity enforces, will vary considerably and will clearly have important implications for the amount and nature of the non-coerced (respondent) behaviour which can appear. A sewing group dominated by its separate, and clattering sewing machines, an art group tied to its isolated canvasses and easels, or a fell-walking group strung out in single file on a narrow path, will interact in one (rather restricted) way. The same group beading a single garment, producing a mural or strolling across easy open country, will set up very different (probably much more fluid) patterns of inter-action.

A group's 'work' in fact, inevitably does much to determine such things as group members' physical proximity, the amount of noise they make (and so how easy or difficult verbal communication is), and individuals' preoccupation with specialised functions, (and so, how available for exchanges with others they are). Each of these may so seriously affect interaction that a worker may need to be extremely aware of them, and plan for them (even perhaps to the point of changing the activity), if their impact turns out to be significantly detrimental to what the group is intended to achieve.

6. What *rewards* do group members receive, how quickly are they distributed, and how often? A participant's need to derive some reward from his involvement in a group's activity is of course, like most of the other areas so far examined, widely and intuitively recognised within social work. Yet this, too, is often dealt with in a very imprecise and unhelpful way: 'Did the discussion help them to clarify their problems?' we often ask, or 'Did they enjoy their climb to the summit?' Yet some other, quite straightforward but rather more probing questions might need to be raised.

For, in the first place, rewards can be both 'intrinsic' and 'secondary'. Thus, if a group member does put into words anxieties which previously he had barely formulated (even privately), or if he does negotiate a quite difficult rock-face, the consequent reward stems from the fact that he has successfully performed an operation, or a series of operations, directly concerned with the group's ascribed task. In this sense, therefore, the reward can be regarded as intrinsic to the activity.

On the other hand, reward, though very real to him, may not arise from sources so essential to what is being done. The group member may, for example, be praised for discussing his personal problems openly, or he may enjoy the view once he has actually negotiated the rock-face; or in either case he may meet new people whose friendship he comes to value. Moreover, these rewards may accrue whether or not the key tasks (of discussion or rock-climbing) are accomplished successfully, or are felt in themselves to be rewarding.

Thus, for a social worker, the *source* of the rewards derived from an activity may be extremely significant. But so, too, may the speed and range of their *distribution*. For example, not all rewards become available quickly. In some activities, participants have to 'work' long and hard before any reward (and certainly any intrinsic reward) is forthcoming. Walking in misty weather up long, gradually ascending paths, when each rise promises to be the summit but the summit never comes, may for many participants be an activity virtually without reward. So, too, might a discussion which never touches on the problem which for most group members is worrying, even though, as a discussion, it has 'gone very well'. And so, too, as the example earlier (p. 96) from the Day Treatment Centre showed, may much 'community service activity'. Clearly, for many clients, rewards need to be available, not only in terms which have a meaning for them personally, but also with a regularity which enables them to go on being motivated and satisfied.

What is more, the spread of these rewards may be equally important. For many clients a group activity would not be particularly useful if repeatedly only one or two 'stars' accumulated all the rewards that were going. And so, an activity which provides only one, or a very few, intrinsic rewards—such as running a race —may prove very unsuitable however 'valuable in its own right' it may seem to be. Of course, others may be praised for their effort and told that they have also broken the previous record time. But these (secondary) rewards cannot be relied upon, and they may well have very little satisfying meaning for those receiving them.

Analysing activities: its limitations and uses

These, then, are six dimensions of a group's activity which might be assessed by a worker and/or his clients. The actual assessment, of course, is not easy. Clearly, there is no degree of prescriptiveness, control, bodily movement and so on which is right for every situation. A worker may intuitively feel—indeed, this chapter may have at times unwittingly implied—that, say, more, rather than less, interaction is always good, or that rewards should always be readily and equally available. Yet every situation, each group of clients, and each individual within that group, will be different. The meaning which any particular form of an activity has for him, will be highly personal, and may differ significantly from the meanings derived from it by all other participants. None of the dimensions can be assumed to have an absolute value.

Moreover, even the answers which can be given will not be objective or totally reliable. How do you assess the 'level' of prescriptiveness, control, bodily movement or even skill, to say nothing of interaction and rewards, in a human endeavour like a group activity? Where are the tools for measuring these phenomena and how accurate are such measurements going to be in any case? At present, anyway, any decisions taken about the levels which are operating, or which should operate, may rest on a high degree of worker intuition and judgment.

These doubts have, of course, to be added to ones expressed elsewhere in this book about the social work process as a whole. In particular, it seems important to repeat yet again how one-sided the worker's perceptions of the client's personality and situation may be, and how crucial the client's *own* perceptions of these things are. This warning seems particularly important in this context, since this framework for analysing group tasks does, after all, rely almost entirely on the work of Vinter and his colleagues (Vinter, 1967b). And, as one writer has pointed out (Tropp, 1968), Vinter 'sees the group as a means by which the worker can meet individual treatment goals—carefully studied and diagnosed, and prescribed for each member of the group—by unashamedly manipulating the group'.

And yet in spite of all these reservations, the framework for analysing group activity presented in this chapter need not be dismissed out of hand. It cannot provide a blueprint for action, or an objective set of instruments for assessing the activities which do or could go on in groups. But it can take some social workers (and some of their clients, too, in some circumstances) beyond the rather haphazard (almost ideological) choices of activity which they seem often to make at present. In effect, social workers seem frequently to say: 'I have always done this with clients' (discussion); or, 'I've gained personally from doing that in my own leisure-time' (outdoor pursuits); or, 'They say I must now do this new thing' (community service). This may oversimplify the motives involved but surely not the arbitrary way in which many group activities are chosen. A rather more self-conscious and analytical process for making these choices should now be possible. Though the framework outlined in this chapter is by no means the only one available (see in particular Middleman, 1968), it is intended to offer one approach to just this kind of self-conscious analysis.

7

The worker inside and outside the group

The group worker's role: fantasy and reality

In recent years, the whole method of group work has acquired a mystique all of its own within social work which is now fed from many directions. More and more social workers have attended courses on which group 'tutors', 'consultants', 'co-ordinators' or whatever, have remained, for all or most of the time, infuriatingly silent. And social workers who have not actually participated in such courses will undoubtedly have been introduced by those who have, to the folklore and mythology which have now collected round them. The result is a very specific conception of group work, and especially of the role of the group worker which, it is assumed, has universal and absolute relevance.

And so, it seems, the group worker has come to be seen as someone who must be able to live through long and embarrassed or hostile silences, and to ride group members' often bitter, personal attacks. His aloofness and self-control suggest both a mysteriously deep insight into what is happening, and a wide range of slick techniques—often suspiciously labelled 'tricks' by course participants—which get the group to react in quite unexpected, unfamiliar—and uncomfortable—ways. The insights seem rarely to be made explicit or the techniques explained. Group members may therefore depart feeling that they have been in the presence of a manipulative charlatan (in which case, they may conclude, if that is group work, they do not want anything more to do with it). Or, they may decide that what they have witnessed is a supercharged and potentially explosive skill which they themselves could never hope to acquire.

Such a picture of the group worker may seem unfair and distorted to the insider. To the uninitiated or newly initiated, however, it is often only too real, and may have the effect of reducing rather than increasing his confidence and motivation to work in groups. The magic of the training experiences he has been through may be recognised as powerful, and even sometimes as doing great things for the worker's own personal development and self-awareness. Unfortunately, however, he seems repeatedly to feel that he himself has not been touched by it in any practical sense. The great day of flashing revelation and instant initiation has still to dawn.

What often seems to happen, in fact, is that would-be group workers become preoccupied with, and overawed by, the role of group worker as they have seen it played on the courses they have attended, and conclude that no other way of playing it is valid. If, then, they work in groups in any other way—if, say, they make quite regular and direct verbal comments on the topic under discussion rather than on behaviour in the group; or if they introduce or even direct quite active tasks; or if they tell group members something of their private experience, attitudes and feelings—they then feel guilty or incompetent, or ill-disciplined.

In fact, of course, no single, universally applicable style of working in a group exists. A worker may be more conscious of what is happening because he has constructed for himself a framework of concepts and knowledge especially relevant to group situations. And yet, flexibility and adaptability remain at a premium, since an appropriate group work contribution in one group, or at one stage of a group's development, may be totally inappropriate in another group or at another time.

This is not to say, of course, that self-criticism and reappraisal by social workers entering group situations are not needed. Caseworkers may well find that, after operating for most of their time through one-to-one encounters, a group meeting seems extremely complex. With more people involved, more names have to be remembered, more words heard and noted, more non-verbal transmissions received and, above all, more interactions observed and their individual meanings understood. Even in a quite formally structured situation such as a discussion group or a committee meeting, events can be bewilderingly fluid and apparently disorganised. A number of individuals may want to talk or act simultaneously and may only be prevented from doing so if the worker or another group member intervenes very directly, even rudely. The flow of events may be very rapid, and yet it may be uneven and disjointed. As a result, the worker may find it hard to 'hold' a particular focus; or to switch back to a theme given insufficient attention earlier; or to extract and emphasise some particularly significant details from within the total events of the moment. The worker may then feel dissatisfied with his performance because he is reacting too slowly—because he seems to be controlled by, rather than to control or at least to influence, the group's movement.

At times, therefore, caseworkers may have good reasons to feel swamped by the group work situation. This feeling of being out of control will very rarely be seriously harmful to group members. But it may mean that, in an effort to turn the tide, a worker imposes on a group both himself and his conception of what is needed, in a quite rigid way. At that point, he may indeed talk too much or dominate the group's activity, or set goals or norms, or demand roles, which have very little helpful meaning for group members. Opportunities potentially relevant to group members' needs may then be missed or simply blocked off.

Certain general guidelines can therefore be laid out to help a worker redress this balance to some degree:

The more a worker says and does in a group, the less freedom he is leaving himself for listening to what others are saying, or for observing what they are doing.

The more he says and does, the fewer openings there may be for group members to say and do what is especially meaningful for them.

Contributions by a worker are only justified anyway when he has something relevant to say or do, and when this contribution is unlikely to be made by another group member.

In any case, everything that a worker can justifiably say or do, need not be introduced all at once in one, unbroken contribution. Those on the receiving end invariably receive, what is being offered, more slowly than the transmitter can formulate and present it. Appropriately phased and paced contributions are therefore essential.

Factual errors or practical mistakes made by group members do not necessarily have to be corrected immediately or even at all: they are often of far less significance to the person making them than to the 'expert' hearing or observing them.

All this implies that a group worker's focus will need often to be on *who* is talking or acting, and not exclusively on *what* they are doing or saying, or on *how well* they are doing or saying it.

But listing such tips can be counter-productive, since to someone who already doubts his ability as a group worker, they may seem to add up to a doctrine of perfection. Even though such guidelines certainly do not rule out quite frequent and active interventions by the worker, they may imply a degree of insight and self-control which the newcomer to group work feels incapable of achieving.

In the long run, therefore, what is needed is a clearer and more confident grasp by a group worker, not only of group processes, group tasks and their impact (see Chapters 5 and 6), but also of the nature and range of his own key functions. He will still, on the spot, have repeatedly and spontaneously to choose what particular line of action to adopt. But he may at least feel less lost, less without reference points, if he can operate on the basis of this broader understanding.

The authority of the group worker

Of prime importance to these functions is the nature and extent of a social worker's authority in a group—that is, his right, obligation and opportunity to authorise the behaviour of other participants. Once again, this cannot be defined for all times and all occasions. In some groups, it may be considerable and quite blatant—in a prisoners' group, for example, where it may be explicitly laid down by the institution which sanctions the group meeting; or in an adolescent rock-climbing group where the group's task puts members at considerable physical risk; or in a children's playgroup where the participants' immaturity can have a similar implication. In other groups, little authority may be formally allocated to the group worker, at least within the group. And where it does operate, it may do so very subtly, and only by consent of the group members. This can often be seen most clearly in the unattached adolescent groups whom detached youth workers meet, or in many of the indigenous and often autonomous groups like the Community Action Group. And it may also exist in some mainly social groups— like the Wives' Club—once they have established themselves and broken away from their dependence on the sponsoring social worker.

All this suggests that the social worker cannot define his authority in a group in any stereotyped, once-and-for-all way. He may claim that he is 'non-directive', and imply that he has and wants no special right to influence the actions of other group members. If, however, he uses this term to describe *a total style of work*, he gives it a meaning which it can hardly bear. He may try to make himself as self-effacing and as uninfluential as possible, by liberally adopting certain non-directive *techniques*. But it is almost certainly impossible for him to succeed in eliminating his impact completely, especially if he is seen, or if he sees himself, as 'the worker' in the group.

For, as an individual with a role ascribed to him, he cannot ever have total freedom of action. After all, such role ascription will, as we saw in Chapter 5, mean that others will have expectations of how he will behave: *they* will have accepted the implications of his label, even if he has not. And these expectations will certainly extend to what behaviour the social worker can and will authorise, and to what behaviour he cannot and will not—that is, to his authority in the group. Group members may view him in this way because they feel they will then have protection or redress against unhelpful treatment by other group members (as Jenny once suggested in the Physically Handicapped Adolescent Group—see p. 65). Or they may assume that, as a social worker, this individual possesses information and expertise which they need, and which should, and must, direct their subsequent actions. Or they may have other reasons for deferring to him.

Whatever their motives, however, they will to some extent *make* his role for him because of their perceptions and expectations of it. The group worker may have—or may say he has—no *self*-expectations about acting as an authority figure within his ascribed role. And, through actual experience of him as he performs the role, clients may come to modify their expectations of him, perhaps radically. Yet, the subjective expectations of others—the personal meaning they attach to the worker's role—will remain very real and, what is more, may have a profound effect on what these others (the clients) actually do. In their interaction with the worker, therefore, they may force him to act to some degree as a bearer of legitimate authority, whether he wishes to do so or not.

All this, of course, leaves out of account the pressures on a worker from outside the group itself—from his colleagues, employers, the public and so on—to accept the authority functions embodied in his ascribed role. When added to the internal group pressures, they mean that a group worker's claim to be able always to act non-directively—that is, as if he had no special authority—rarely stands up to scrutiny.

This is not to say, however, that the diametrically opposite point of view has any absolute validity. A worker will not necessarily bring order, coherence and meaning to group situations simply by abandoning the 'non-directive' techniques appropriate to case-work. He may be tempted to keep clients in groups on a very tight rein, in order to prevent them from wandering aimlessly through their discussions, or from putting themselves and others involved in their activities in danger, or from failing to fulfil a 'community service' obligation they have taken on. Objectives, and the framework within which action takes place, may then be so rigidly laid down that 'directiveness' becomes a total style of work, rather than, again, a tactical manoeuvre to be adopted at appropriate moments.

For, to react to the demands of a group situation this directively is to waste many of the opportunities for offering help which a group can provide. The potentiality of group experience as outlined, for example, in Chapter 4 is very unlikely to be realised if the worker feels he must unrelentingly move group members towards ends which he, and only he, prescribes. How often in such a situation will individuals be able to act as helpers *to each other*? How strongly, even, will they identify with each other, as people sharing common problems and capable of working collectively towards common goals? Even in the casework situation, the worker needs always to be wary of assuming that he is the most useful and effective resource in a client's life. In a group, such an assumption is, as we have seen, even less reliable. Moreover, it is even less necessary. For group situations invariably allow clients actually to experience fellow-clients, and the worker, in new ways.

The worker outside the group

What, then, might the group worker's functions be? Undoubtedly, his contribution to the life of a group can begin even before he actually meets the group as a group. This is particularly true of course when the group is deliberately formed by a worker within an agency framework. But it may apply, too, at least in part, even when the group has existed prior to, and totally independently of, the worker's intervention.

For, the impact of the 'external system' of a group (Homans, 1951) on its internal life and social organisation can be extremely subtle. In a social work context, some of the most important features of this external system may include:

1. *The attitudes of the agency in general and of the worker's colleagues and superiors in particular* In agencies where group work is well established, the attitudes of superiors and colleagues may hardly seem to be an issue. In many others, however, group work may still at best be a peripheral, and even a trendy, extra. Workers therefore have frequently to introduce group work in the form of a special 'project' or 'experiment'. This of course may be welcomed, though regarded with some curiosity. However, most modern social work agencies are, in practice, middle- or large-scale bureaucratic organisations. And such organisations are not renowned for their responsiveness to new ideas and methods, and may, by their very nature, teach 'hidden' lessons which are in direct

conflict with the experiences which a group work approach is meant to provide (Klein, 1970), pp. 98-104). Efforts to introduce group work into them may therefore be greeted negatively, or even with downright hostility, and may constantly be in danger of having their stated goals displaced.

An overwhelmingly negative reaction poses the would-be group worker with at least two major sets of functions. One requires him to operate at a 'political' level within the agency, to ensure that some group work activity can at least begin. Initially, this may *not* mean trying to modify underlying attitudes to group work. These may not be susceptible to direct pressures relying mainly on theoretical arguments in favour of group work. Rather, they may only begin to alter after colleagues and superiors have had some actual *experience* within their agency of the usefulness of group work, as well, of course as of its *actual* limitations. A group worker may thus have to press ahead despite a mainly unsympathetic external environment, and protect himself and the group as far as he can from the pressures that result.

But such an approach will also require a worker to deepen his understanding of how bureaucratic organisations operate (see, for example, Blau and Scott, 1963; and Smith, 1970) and, in the light of these insights, to define his role, at least in part, as a change agent within his own organisation. This may involve, for example, identifying those parts (people, procedures, administrative machinery and so on) of his agency which are sufficiently open and flexible to permit some experiment, however limited. And it may mean accepting certain compromises so that, for example, he starts his group work programme rather less ambitiously than he might originally have envisaged.

A group's external and internal systems will, however, be much more directly related and interdependent than this may suggest. A second, no less difficult set of functions for a group worker, therefore, will involve him in mediating between his agency and the (perhaps emergent) internal organisation of the group. The overall emphasis here may be a protective one : to group members, he may never openly acknowledge the external system and its pressures, and may even build whatever barriers he can between the two. These barriers may be blatantly physical—he may meet the group away from the agency's premises, or at least in a single, separate room with a tightly closed door. Timings may also be used to restrict direct agency-group contact to a minimum, as may many of the tasks pursued by the group.

On the other hand, the worker may try deliberately to carry forward the group's development, at least in part, by facing the group members with as much of the external system as they can cope with directly. Dealing with the agency's attitude to group work, and trying to alter it, may then become one of the tasks of the group. And this may have non-verbal as well as verbal features: what the group *does* within (or indeed, to) the agency, and in whose presence it does it, may be at least as influential as what is said. The mere failure to fulfil staff expectations of noise or vandalism or disruption may reduce agency resistance.

> Mr Jenks, the Head, came into the hall just as the fight scene was reaching its crescendo, and stayed on right through the hospital scene. At first, he looked very uncomfortable, and maybe even disapproving, and the kids were obviously very aware of his presence. I, too, suddenly became very conscious again of the amount of noise they were making during the fight and had to repress an urge to step in and quieten them down, especially since they seemed to be dealing with their embarrassment by making even more noise than usual. . . . Afterwards, Mr Jenks called me into his office. He commented on the youngsters' enthusiasm, and also on the standard of acting. He is apparently quite unaware of, or uninterested in, the personal gains the kids are making through their drama, but at least he now seems much less suspicious of what we're doing, and even quite tolerant of it. However, he still managed to make a very cutting comment about Debbie (Physically Handicapped Adolescent Group).

A worker's actual exercise of this function may on occasions be complicated by the fact that other colleagues join him as co-workers in a group. Such a division of authority may anyway be confusing for group members. This in itself can be made productive, especially if it mirrors other group situations which individuals meet outside the agency and in which such role confusion is present. However, before they actually enter the group, the workers do usually need to acknowledge the *fact* of this division to each other. They may also need to agree on a division of labour, so that the group's formal goals can be pursued with some clarity and coherence. This is normally accepted very readily where, as in rock-climbing, the group's instrumental task involves some possible physical danger. It is usually agreed less quickly, if at all, in, say, a discussion group, camp group, community group, or social club. Here, two, three or even more workers may be present, each acting as if he were the only one so labelled.

Such an unplanned use of divided authority may have one particularly significant consequence: it may allow conflicts and tensions to be played out in a group whose roots are to be found right outside the group, within the agency at large. Struggles for dominance in a group 'led' by more than one worker may be explicable only in terms of such outside pressures. This fact alone therefore suggests that divided authority requires the workers involved to undertake some very special preparation for their group meetings. And this in turn might be seen as a specific example of the more general need for a worker to function both in the client group and also in its external environment, and perhaps also to mediate between the two.

2. *A newly-formed group's size and composition* Mediation between the internal and external systems of a social work group will probably occur, however, over quite specific issues. A good example of this is when a new group is being formed and the worker concerned is forced to negotiate with colleagues over which of 'their' clients might join him.

However, issues such as group size and composition are important in their own right, and point to a further set of functions for the group worker. On occasions, of course, a worker may have little room for manoeuvre over the size of his group. Thus, within the agency, the actual number of 'eligible' candidates for group membership may be limited. Alternatively, numbers may be laid down for him quite rigidly by the very nature of the task: only eleven or twelve people (and usually only boys or men, at that) can normally play in a competitive football game. Alternatively, safety factors may suggest an optimum number—for example, in rock-climbing. Or the need for essential equipment—say tents for a camping expedition, or canoes for canoeing practice—may impose a limit. A group worker may be tempted sometimes to ignore some of these limits, or to stretch them unrealistically. But, in doing this, he may leave certain group members uninvolved or underinvolved in the group's instrumental task. Considerable respondent behaviour (see Chapter 6) may then result, which effectively blocks progress towards the group's formal goals.

These examples do assume that the formal goals concerned are largely focused on acquiring and developing recreational interests and skills. What, however, if the group is intended primarily to release individual tensions, or to develop a sense of identity among group members, or to nurture their social skills and a greater personal control over their own lives? If a worker is then able to exercise considerable discretion over how many people should join the group, how best might he use it?

As a general principle, decisions about group size in situations like this are likely to be appropriate only if they are carefully related to the predominantly *expressive* purposes set for the groups. For, in such groups, the emergence of trust and intimacy among group members may be absolutely essential. A key function of the worker may therefore be to create optimum conditions for this to happen. If the group is too small, individuals may feel under too great a pressure to reveal themselves personally. They may then very quickly put up barriers to personal statement (verbal and non-verbal) which, even later, may be difficult or impossible to breach. On the other hand, in a group which is too large, a number of individuals may want, and be able, to remain emotionally hidden and socially inactive. For them, therefore, the outcome may be the opposite of what the worker intended.

Many of the same considerations may operate when the question to be resolved is no longer, *How many* group members should there be? but, *Who* should be invited to join? Thus, if performing a recreational task well—say, winning football matches or becoming a skilled rock-climber—is not a high priority, then it may be possible to make mere ability to participate, the sole criterion for joining. If, on the other hand, a high level of performance is an important priority, then selection criteria may need to be much more restrictive. Only in that way may individual frustrations and unhelpful respondent behaviour in the group be kept well under control.

Where more expressive tasks are central to the group, then other principles may need to guide individuals' introduction to it. Relevant questions then may be:

How far do potential group members have emotional or social concerns in common before they enter the group? (These concerns might be categorised as, for example, problems, interests, aspirations, self-expectations, type of offence, etc.)

Might these individuals eventually, even if not immediately, be able to deal more openly (whether verbally or through action) with these concerns? Or might they respond to the public situation of the group either by withdrawing completely, or by continually blocking others' efforts at overt identification and action?

Do the individuals concerned have a minimum capacity to delay personal gratification while the group organises its instrumental tasks and its social transactions?

The most that the worker might expect from such a check-list is a series of rather crude guidelines for finding his way through a highly complex and basically unpredictable situation. Even this, however, does not convey adequately the most fundamental, and intrinsic weakness of any selection process: that it may simply repeat and reinforce both a worker's perceptions of 'the client' and also perhaps the client's perceptions of himself. These perceptions may of course be helpful. Often, however, they will not. Indeed, some of them may be so negative that they may actually prevent clients' development. They may cast him in roles which make a fresh and more autonomous expression of the self difficult, even impossible. A person may be judged as being incapable of performing certain recreational or other tasks, even though there is no overriding physical reason for making the judgment. Or he may be seen as bound to meet frustration and failure when faced with certain social situations or certain emotional demands, even though such conclusions may merely contribute to, if not actually ensure, the very outcomes they predict; they may in fact merely be key elements of a very subtle self-fulfilling process. The question which always needs to be borne in mind, therefore, is: How far does a worker's selection of clients for group membership reproduce and strengthen the labels which are already attached to those clients and which may in themselves be contributing to their problems. Selection may be a necessary and crucial step in forming a group capable of fulfilling certain stated aims. But it can also be a means of evading the interactional difficulties jointly faced by clients and agency. Often, anyway, of course, a worker has little or no opportunity (or right) to influence who will belong to a particular group. Specially formed groups with a recreational focus, or with single-mindedly, expressive goals, are not, as this book has repeatedly stressed, by any means the only ones through which social workers might operate. Some groups will adopt tasks which are even more closely related to the very practical events and situations of clients' everyday lives—to their functions as parents, or as residents of a neighbourhood, or as alcoholics or persistent offenders or adolescents with physical handicaps. A worker's control of group composition may then be very weak or non-existent. And, where it does operate, it will often be guided by some very obvious, and perhaps imposed, considerations. (For a rather more worker-centred view of group formation and composition see Hartford, 1972 Chapter 4.)

3. *A group's physical field of operation* Group workers may in practice have little if any opportunity to influence a group's physical field of operation. Its major features may certainly be out-

side their control—for example, the actual building to be used—while even the precise room or the furnishings or equipment available—may be dictated to them. Nonetheless, even within these limitations, some freedom for worker and clients will clearly often exist. Thus, it may be possible, at least to some extent, to control the lighting in a room, so that, according to group purposes, it encourages or discourages intimate discussion or extrovert activity. Similarly, decisions about furniture and its arrangements are often open to the worker and the group's members. They might effect, not only how the chairs are arranged—in a circle, semi-circle, round a fire, and so on—but also whether tables are retained as a form of emotional (or even physical) protection for those taking part.

This adaptation of the physical environment can be subtle, and may have some quite valuable effects on a group's social organisation. Thus, a discussion group need not be *only* a discussion group. Relevant books or magazines left lying out, or paper and pencils for doodling and drawing, can often enable words to flow more easily and freely. Similarly, as the Community Home Girls' Group showed (p. 50), an activity which draws people together round a table, and occupies their hands and minds but still leaves them periods free to think of other matters, can also release tongues. Such discussion may often be sprawling and at least partly out of the worker's direct control, or it may sometimes occur within sub-groups simultaneously pursuing rather different lines. Such untidiness does not, however, mean it is valueless.

Similarly, an activity group need not be *only* an activity group. It may also, because of the opportunities provided within its physical area of operation, be a very coherent discussion group. This may depend on how the instrumental tasks of the group—its baking, its hill-climbing, its acting—are organised. Do they allow individuals to come into close physical proximity with each other? Or do they keep them apart, or even place barriers between them? Do they place participants facing each other or in opposite directions? Do they require them to share or exchange equipment? And so on.

4. *A group's use of time*   In group work, rigid ideas about the use of time can be difficult to maintain. With more people involved in a group meeting, the chances of there being more latecomers anyway are correspondingly higher. In addition, if a worker insists on starting strictly on time—neither before nor after the set hour—he must accept that on each occasion *he* must use a quite formal opening gambit. This, of course, may be appropriate in many

groups. But in others he may have a choice. While group members are still arriving, he may be able to make an unobtrusive move into the group's task, whether this is primarily verbal or non-verbal.

This may in addition have a useful side-effect: it may demonstrate that the worker sees group members as individuals first and as group members only second. To await the arrival of all or most of the other members could be taken by those already present to mean that *their* interests and needs are not of concern to him in their own right, but only in the context of the group. Indeed, if the others never arrive and the worker questions whether it is worth continuing at all, he may even end up implying that those who have come have, for him, no individual significance whatsoever.

Decisions about endings as well as beginnings may also have to be made even prior to a group meeting. If it is a formal or semi-formal gathering, will there be any break part-way through and if so, when; and how will it be indicated and by whom? How strictly will the set time for finishing be enforced anyway? In some groups, practical circumstances may mean this has to be done rigidly—mothers may have to collect children from school, adolescents may have to be home by a certain hour, an institution may lay down certain strict limits. In others—community action or camp groups—flexibility may be much more important, and the worker may anyway have little control over the situation.

5. Communicating the group's purpose and the worker's role to group members Where a group is starting from scratch, a group may be puzzled about, and even suspicious of, its purpose and the role the worker will play. After all, the initiative will almost certainly have been taken by a person in authority whose actions will often have a different meaning for clients from that intended by the worker himself. What he offers as a therapeutic and supportive experience may, for the client, appear as punitive (see Phil's comment—p. 86—on the Boys' Camp Group mountain climb), or as controlling and restrictive (see the Day Treatment Centre decorating exercise, p. 96) or even, as the Physically Handicapped Adolescent Group seemed to imply on one occasion (p. 86), as primarily exploratory, even prying. The worker cannot therefore assume that the group's goals, or the nature of his own participation, will be self-evident to would-be members.

And so, even before a group meets he may have to function as a communicator and interpreter. In this, he faces considerable problems. In the first place, his contact with potential participants will not always be first-hand: they may be new to the agency or 'belong' to other workers. In any case, the worker will be trying to convey what the group is for, and the gains it might bring those who join it, in advance of their actual *experience* of these things. He will thus be relying on communicating intellectually and second-hand, something which is undoubtedly significant mainly because of its emotional and personal meaning and impact. In practice, of course, he stands only a slight chance of doing this satisfactorily. Yet, at the very least, he must by his efforts raise sufficient motivation and confidence in individuals who may be very uncertain and isolated, to ensure that they take a (for them) quite risky first step.

A worker entering a group already in existence faces a somewhat similar dilemma. He must by some means make himself and *his* purposes tolerable and eventually positively acceptable within a social organisation which pre-dates his intervention. Those who work with adolescent friendship groups, and again especially the detached youth worker, know this problem in an acute form. On occasions, they have evaded it by disguising their identity and purposes. They have then insinuated themselves into groups as if they did not have an ascribed role, or as if that ascribed role was other than that of 'social group worker' (see, for example, Morse, 1965).

Normally, however, they have faced the problem head-on whenever it has been relevant to do so. They have then introduced themselves as youth workers, or social workers and have made their 'helping' intentions explicit. (See, for example, Goetschius and Tash, 1967; Smith, Farrant and Marchant, 1972.) Some have even used the exchanges generated by this direction to *demonstrate* why they are there rather than merely talking about this (Button, 1967, pp. 6-10; and 1971, pp. 31-4).

The precise mode of achieving this communication, as in all such matters, can thus vary a great deal. A key principle, however, is almost certainly that what a group worker *says* is likely to be much less convincing to group members than what he does. One important function for the worker, therefore, is, prior to meeting a group, to bring as many of the potential members as he can to a point where this practical demonstration of his intentions and functions can begin. He may *assume* that they will know why they are coming or that they want to come simply because, in writing or verbally in a one-to-one situation, they have had the group's aim explained to them. This, however, is to fail to recognise the complexity of initial and abstract communications. And it will almost certainly make the first experiences frustrating and unsatisfactory for all those taking part. As we saw in the last chapter, starting where group members are when they first join a group may thus often mean starting with their confusions and suspicions about the very group situation in which they find themselves. Anticipating what this starting-point may be, trying to touch it prior even to the clients' joining a group meeting, and certainly preparing to connect and negotiate with it when they first come together, represent key functions for a worker in advance of a group session. Communication of purpose is thus a key part of establishing the contact between worker and group members, which means it can only be achieved within the interactional processes of the group itself (Klein, 1970, pp. 50-2).

Targets for intervention within the group

Once a worker is in personal contact with a group, a variety of possible targets for his intervention may be available. In other words, there exist a number of potentially significant areas of group experience to which a worker can relate himself in constructive ways. These areas include:

Group members' *practical and technical management* of their key instrumental tasks

Group members' *cognitive* awareness and understanding of themselves and their situation

Group members' organisation of their *social* transactions and especially of the way they control these transactions

The *affective* (feeling) results of these transactions

Though, once again, separating these areas is an artificial exercise, each does require more detailed examination in its own right.

1. Group members' practical and technical management of their key instrumental tasks Instrumental tasks—those actions intended to be instrumental in achieving a group's ascribed goals—may, as we have seen, include anything from talking in a discussion group, to brewing a cup of tea in a mothers' social club, canvassing for signatures for a petition, or producing an improvised piece of drama. The last chapter emphasised, above all, that a worker's influence on these tasks could be considerable. The question which remains is: How can this influence be exercised?

In the first place, of course, a worker may well be in a position to decide which, and how many, material and human resources crucial to the task's development will actually be made available to the group. Not only money, but also vehicles, kitchenware, tape-recorders, projectors, cameras, ropes, canoes, maps, books and so on, plus people with the expertise to use such resources—all of these may be at the *direct* disposal only of the worker. Deciding whether, when and how to make these available represents a key form of worker intervention in a group's practical management of its instrumental tasks. It also gives the worker very great, if often unacknowledged, power to influence group members and the satisfactions they derive from a group.

Clearly, however, this influence may also extend into non-material spheres of group life, in particular because of the technical expertise which a worker may bring to it. For, he will himself often have skills and knowledge which could be useful, even essential, to the work a group has in hand.

For those unsure of their functions in a group—including, apparently, many social workers—this form of intervention may seem particularly attractive. Thus, they may be continually tempted to provide verbal clarifications and theoretical interpretations of what has been said in discussion; or to coach group members in the finer skills of negotiating a rock-face; or to lobby personally on behalf of the client pressure group.

Such contributions may of course be essential; they may, for example, be expected or required by the group members themselves, who would feel cheated or patronised if the worker did not make them. But they *may* have more to do with the worker's need to find a clear and satisfying function for himself. And even when relevant, they may have lasting social and emotional side-effects on a group and on the development of its social organisation. Participants other than the worker may, for example, never have the chance to play significant 'technical' roles. The person who, himself, consistently clarifies, corrects, coaches, and negotiates may come to be seen as the only person who does these things—and, perhaps also, as the person who does *only* these things. Moreover, while doing them, he will not cease to be an emotionally and socially significant 'other' in the group—a figure of some importance and sway, whose attention, approval, and support carry special weight. Thus, *whose* view he chooses to clarify or interpret, *whom* he chooses to coach and praise, on *whose* behalf he chooses to negotiate, will all be noted and judged by group members. Group members' *self*-perceptions and *self*-expectations, and the perceptions and expectations individual members hold of *each other*, may thus be subtly, but crucially, influenced and their transactions with each other correspondingly altered. Is the worker aware of the interactional repercussions of his practical and technical activity?

Pete was another of the boys who had never ever been near a

rock-face before, but he showed an immediate flair for what was required. Without being cocky like Phil, he showed much less fear than the others, and grasped the instructions I gave to him very quickly. In a short afternoon, he made some real progress and was very enthusiastic to keep trying.... As we left to get back into the cars, Phil (who was walking just a little way ahead with Mark) said something like: 'You can tell who's the blue-eyed boy now, can't you?', and they both laughed. From the direction of their glance, I assumed they were talking about Pete (Boys' Camp Group).

The discussion by now seemed to be well and truly bogged down: no-one seemed very clear on the best way to get Mr Grey, the relevant official at the town hall, to come and meet the group. As a last resort, I therefore suggested that I ring him and try to persuade him myself. Mr Wright, Mr Henry and Mr Raymond received the idea enthusiastically, in fact it seemed with relief, and it was quickly agreed by the whole committee.... As I left the meeting, Mrs Baker stopped me and said quietly: 'So, you've joined the enemy, have you?' I didn't understand what she meant at first, but then she added: 'That man Grey coming is a waste of time. The more we hob-nob with the town hall, the less we'll get done.' Apparently, bogging the discussion down had been the way she and one or two others had tried to block the invitation to Grey! (Community Action Group)

2. *Group members' cognitive awareness and understanding of themselves and their situation*   In the past, the training of caseworkers has usually stressed the importance of clients clarifying who they are and where they are via verbalisation and rational analysis. Words, ordered thoughts and intellectually guided reactions, it is implied, are perhaps the most effective tools for changing oneself and one's personal relationships, especially when these are strained. Thus, clients' *cognitive* processes—what they *know*, and consciously *understand* and think, even about their own *emotions*, have thus constituted a major target of casework intervention.

As a result, much social work intervention in groups is liable to have a similar emphasis. Whatever a group's *stated* instrumental task, a very high premium may be placed on explicit discussion of members' problems and behaviour, personality traits and capacities, motives and feelings. Not only discussion groups *per se*, but also groups meeting for practical or social or recreational reasons, may be seen as needing to produce intensive, introspective verbal exchanges in order to justify their existence.

The capacity to achieve such cognitive clarification is of course one of the distinguishing features of human beings. So also is the ability to express such private cognitive processes publicly, in words. Moreover, as this book has emphasised repeatedly, if individuals are firmly labelled in advance by a 'significant other' as, say, inarticulate or non-rational, then their actual presentation of themselves to that 'other' is liable to be predetermined in quite important ways. Thus, cognitive activity needs always to be viewed as potentially helpful and relevant to members of social work groups.

Nonetheless, an unrelenting, almost exclusive focusing on cognitive appraisal of oneself and one's situation can on many occasions be unproductive, or even counter-productive. It can highlight individuals' self-consciousness (especially when with authority figures) and produce primarily the verbal responses which, it is felt, the authority figure expects.

In fact, especially in the context of group work, social workers' emphasis on verbal expression and responses raises a number of critical questions. Are cognitive processes the only, or even the main, means by which individuals learn and develop? What if, as again this book has argued repeatedly, changing a person's self-perceptions and self-expectations can lead to significant changes in their behaviour and in their capacity to control their own lives? What if *others'* perceptions and expectations are continually reinforcing or remaking these individual self-images? And what if this flow and counter-flow of perceptions and expectations depends to a major extent on what people *do* in each other's presence—on how they behave and on how others behave towards them—rather than primarily on what they *say* to each other? What priority then should be given to verbalised, rational clarifications—to cognitive appraisals—of an individual's problems and potentialities? Might not more stress be placed by social workers on trying to influence what individuals *experience* with, and of, each other—on how they control each other, what they do together, who they do it with, and so on?

Thus, social work activity aimed at making these *experiences* more satisfying and developmental might often prove particularly productive in the lives of individual clients, almost whatever the verbal content of those experiences. The worker's encouragement of the hospital scene in the Physically Handicapped Adolescent Group's improvisation (p. 98) would surely be one example of this. So, too, might a worker's public reaction to Mrs Williams when she appeared at the Wives' Club in her best clothes (p. 41); or to Bill's unusually accepting attitude to Jamie, the alcoholic, at the Day Treatment Centre (p. 39). (See also Phillips, 1957, pp. 145-7.) For, these incidents show how a worker can deliberately work to create experiences out of which personal learning can be derived; and also how he can endorse equally positive experiences which arise without his prompting.

None of this is meant to suggest that a group's exchanges at a cognitive level are irrelevant to social work practice, or that they should not constitute a target for it. It is merely intended to redress balance—which in social work often seems to be tipped in favour of the saying and the knowing, and away from the doing and the experiencing.

3. Group members' organisation of their social transactions, and especially of the way they control these transactions Clearly, redressing the balance in this way must have one important outcome: it must make those *social* experiences which help to create and re-create an individual's image and expectations of himself a prime target for social work intervention. Thus, often, rather than simply intervening directly in the verbal exchanges of a group, a worker may need to try to utilise and influence the many other types of interactions which are occurring around him.

No doubt, in many casework situations, opportunities for exerting this type of influence also exist: no interview, as we know, is conducted entirely via words. However, in such situations, the instrumental task is usually restricted primarily to discussion. Also, the number of 'selves' and 'others' taking part is limited, as is the number of versions of these which any participant can present.

In a group, however, a worker is almost certain to have many more opportunities for intervening deliberately in the non-verbal, experiential exchanges which take place among individuals. In this context, 'experience' is intended to mean much more than simply 'doing an activity'—discussing, climbing mountains, drinking tea and so on. It is intended also to include the experience of *being* and of *transacting socially* with others. Or, to adopt terminology used in an earlier chapter, when we talk of a worker influencing group members' experience, we are implying that he should make the group's emerging social organisation a major target of his intervention.

In this, rules (norms) governing what is correct and permissible behaviour may be particularly significant. For, the worker, by reason of his ascribed role and the authority embedded in this, will usually be a most 'significant other' in the group, whether this significance is felt by the client to be positive or negative. And, as such, he will have a special need, and perhaps also some extra opportunities and resources, for *legitimising* certain types of behaviour, and rendering other types illegitimate.

And so, as a group develops, the norms controlling not just how the task is carried out but also how participating individuals are treated, may *prevent* new experiences occurring. Individuals who, say, try on new roles, and thereby risk themselves to some extent, may, if they err, be punished. They may be punished even for trying. The punishment may be direct, or it may be indirect—for example, it may take the form of ridicule, rejection, or their being forced to take on unpleasant or unrewarding tasks. (After his display of enthusiasm for rock-climbing, and Phil and Mark's reaction to it, Pete, as well as the worker, may be particularly at risk in this way. Unwritten rules about what to do and with whom, and with what degree of commitment, may all have been broken. Some attempt by Phil to exert sanctions may therefore be inevitable.)

In fact, a group may state or imply, not just that the *specific* forms of behaviour are unacceptable, but that trying out, risking, experimenting *as such* are 'illegitimate'. And this may be especially true when, through such behaviour, an individual seeks to alter his own self-image, his self-presentation and some of the group members' mutual expectations. While group members are synchronising their social techniques, or emphasising their instrumental tasks, *any* behaviour is liable to be punished, especially if individuals reveal where they are vulnerable. Once a routine and structure have been established, non-conformity becomes a threat to the group's new-found security and may therefore still be severely sanctioned.

Thus, as we saw earlier (p. 41), a worker may, by his own verbal and non-verbal contribution, have to demonstrate that he at any rate does not regard experimentation, or the 'errors' it can produce, as impermissible in themselves. More positively, his function may often have to be to support, again non-verbally as well as verbally, those actions which reach out for new experience and those individuals who attempt some new self-presentation. This will, perhaps, be particularly important in the later stages of a group's development. For, having achieved a degree of stability, the group may be inclined to settle for what it has, rather than use its new-found internal resources to encourage forms of 'deviational allowance' (see p. 41.).

By this time, Alf and Don were losing concentration, especially since their clay wasn't moist enough and their models kept falling apart. It was also getting to 12.30 and lunch-time and, as it was Thursday, they were obviously hoping that all three of them might be able to get away for a quick drink. However, Fred was still thoroughly absorbed in what he was doing and had even begun to sculpt a face in the clay. Alf asked him: 'What's that supposed to be?', and his voice contained more than a trace of mockery. Don laughed and the two of them then began to make a series of sarcastic comments about 'another Picasso' and 'perhaps the art gallery would buy it'. Fred seemed to hesitate for a moment in what he was doing, so I leaned over and made a suggestion about how to improve the eyes and eyebrows. He tried out my suggestion for a few minutes, then said: 'I'll come back to it after dinner', and left the room with Alf and Don (Day Treatment Centre).

Thus, a key target of worker intervention may often need to be the *normative* facets of group interaction. The worker's function then, by both verbal and non-verbal means, will be to help legitimise certain types of behaviour and to try and render other types illegitimate, or at least less acceptable.

In this context, 'non-verbal' clearly has to be defined very broadly. It will, as can be seen from the above example, include what a worker does directly within the instrumental activity of a group—that is, *the way* he discusses, coaches clay-modelling or rock-climbing or helps organise petitions. But it will also include more personal elements of the worker's behaviour, such as whether, and how far, he conveys his own uncertainties and limitations in the task, and therefore how ready he himself is to risk himself, to experiment. And to ask how openly he acknowledges and deals with his own mistakes and failures. The worker's own behaviour, too, will communicate what weight is given to excellence and competence, and how far those who, even marginally, fail to attain the ideal deserve rejection, even of the most courteous kind. Does the worker, in fact, by his presentations of *himself* in the group, help establish norms which support the new client self-presentations and self-images which, he claims, he is in business to promote?

After lunch, Alf, Don and Fred returned to the clay-modelling, and Miss T, who had been away at court all morning, wandered in to see what was happening. She immediately began to fiddle with the clay, making a somewhat half-hearted effort to mould it into the shape of a bowl. Like Alf, and Don earlier, she had great trouble making it stick, and this somehow made her attitude more serious and more determined. Alf, who was also fashioning a sort of bowl, by now had something to show for his efforts, and he and Fred (still working on his head) began to poke fun at Miss T. They suggested half-seriously to me that

I give her some advice as she obviously needed it. Miss T laughed with them, but also listened very carefully when I did give her advice and also sought advice off Alf on one or two occasions. By the end of the next hour, all four of them had progressed far enough for them to ask that what they'd done be locked away so they could carry on with it next week (Day Treatment Centre).

A flexible normative structure which permits personal risk and experimentation could, for the social worker, have a further, tactical advantage: it could help establish a more flexible role structure. As we have seen, performing a group's tasks demands some division of labour among those taking part. The 'labour' which is divided is both that done on the group's instrumental tasks and also that which is concerned with establishing and maintaining some form of social organisation within the group—that is, with its expressive tasks.

In both the instrumental and expressive spheres, this role structure can be extremely rigid. If the task is, say, discussion, group members will often know, or believe they know, who will most often supply information, ask factual questions, clarify what has been said, recall past thoughts, link separate contributions, express personal opinions and so on. They may have similarly fixed preconceptions about who will relieve tensions (perhaps by making a joke or changing the subject), who will protect group members under pressure, who will most often need this protection, who will ease the entry of a reserved individual, who will block such a move, and so on.

In this way, expectations and self-expectations of how individuals within the group will behave can become set. Moreover, in a rather circular process, individuals' subsequent behaviour may, as we have seen, reinforce these expectations and set them even more firmly. Such a rigid role structure can clearly prevent experimentation. Thus, individuals can find it difficult to experience themselves acting in any new ways, or to present themselves to others afresh. Many groups thus develop a whole range of self-fulfilling prophecies about individuals and their roles, which are built deeply into the organisation of their social transactions (see for example, Button, 1969).

Here, then, is a potentially most significant target of intervention by a group worker. Loosening up a group's normative controls over individuals' behaviour may, as a side effect, give those individuals greater freedom to try on new roles. However, at this point, the worker will almost certainly be in a chicken-and-egg situation. For, if by other means, he (or any other group member, of course) is able anyway to modify the role structure that exists, he may succeed in making the norms less restrictive for those seeking a deviational allowance. In other words, new forms of self-presentation which do not destroy the group, and may even make it more rewarding for all concerned, may significantly alter the rules governing group behaviour.

What means, then, of modifying a set role structure are available to the worker, or to group members generally? Once again, the worker's contributions—practically, organisationally, technically —to the group's instrumental tasks may be crucial. The format and context of these tasks may at times be most susceptible to change. The physical features of the environment, for example, may on occasions force individuals into fixed types of contribution. The mere lay-out and equipment and furniture may discourage physical movement and so prevent individuals devising new forms of labour or dividing it in new ways. Or it may prevent sub-groups from forming, in which alternative expectations and self-expectations could emerge. Or again, as was suggested earlier, discussion might on some occasions be supplemented or even replaced by another task—likely clay-modelling or improvised drama. Or, books and magazines might be left lying around so that reading or looking at relevant pictures becomes a passing task, or even an important stimulant, at least for some group members. (For an excellent illustration of this see Maier, 1965, pp. 57-78.) By applying some of the insights into tasks and their intrinsic structure outlined in the last chapter, a worker might not just enable group members to *do* different things; he might also encourage them to begin to expect new forms of behaviour, both of themselves and of others—that is, to play new roles.

Such encouragement has, at least by implication, been present in some of the case material quoted in this book. It perhaps lay behind the worker's response: 'Yes, I'm sure that Ellen would understand that' when, in the Community Home Girls' Group, Fran collapsed in tears (p. 40); and also in the worker's public compliment to Mrs Williams, of the Wives' Club, on how well her dress fitted her (p. 41). And it could certainly be seen in Miss T's change of the role to that of learner, and her acceptance of Alf in the role of teacher, during the Day Training Centre's clay-modelling session (p. 124). On the other hand, though this encouragement has probably also been present in other incidents which have been described (see for example the rock-climbing session of the Boys' Camp Group, p. 119), it has apparently had results which, according to the values and goals held by the social workers, can only be described as negative or counter-productive.

Indeed, it is undeniable that the interrelations of the various elements of a group's organisation are extremely complex. Any change in one—in norms, tasks, roles or whatever—is almost bound to bring often unexpected changes in the others, which may or may not be in the control of a worker, or of anyone else.

However, the group worker, above all, needs to be aware that change in individuals is not brought about only by what they think and know. It may occur, too, as a result of what they experience. And influential experience may arise, not only out of doing an activity. It may also come because each group member is relating to the other *while* he is doing that activity. In particular, such experience can change self-images, and the images individuals hold of each other, and could therefore trigger new behaviour in those who are interacting. Thus, the *means* in group work may be the group's instrumental activity—that is, the actual work the group does. But the *target* for the group worker's intervention will often need to be the group's organisation of its personal and expressive transactions.

4. The affective (feeling) results of these transactions The emotional impact on group members of their social transactions can, as we saw in Chapter 5, be considerable. Though we may, for analytical purposes, talk about individuals 'organising their relationships', in reality they never interact with each other as if they were mere cogs in some carefully controlled and serviced mechanism. Inevitably, they will have feelings about entering a group which will often be strong and may also be mixed. And throughout members' involvement in the group, these and other sensations will repeatedly 'interfere' with their reception of what is being communicated around them.

For, as we have seen, what group members experience is not simply what a detached outsider may observe or judge as central to events. It is in large measure what filters through the feelings which stand between the receiver and the social world (in this case, 'the group') to which he belongs. As a result, what he does is, in the eyes of the 'detached observer', frequently unpredictable, or even 'disfunctional'.

Thus, learning and re-learning, which is what modifying images and self-images involves, can never be achieved in an emotional vacuum. Those who want to help this learning must—as the case material quoted has repeatedly demonstrated—continually aim at shaping an emotional environment which positively generates, rather than blocks or even merely permits, new and perhaps risky forms of self-presentation. What tasks, they are forced to ask, with which individuals playing which roles, may make group members initially feel more secure, more motivated, more willing to invest more of their hidden selves in this group?

The simple 'ice-breaker' events which group workers often use quite intuitively when a group first meets—certain types of games with children (and even adults), pop music for adolescents, cups of tea and biscuits for harassed mothers—are clearly examples of this type of intervention. They start, and attempt to connect, with where individuals are *emotionally* rather than intellectually or even socially. And their focus is where individuals are emotionally *within* the group as well as outside it.

If an individual's security and motivation in a group does grow, it will almost certainly mean that he has acquired a sense of identity with other individuals in the group. For this to happen—for individuals to feel 'there is something of me in them and them in me'—group members will (once again) need, not just *to be told* of their mutuality, but also *to share experiences* which enable them to discover it for themselves. These experiences will have to be valued by those who share them, and they will have actually to *demonstrate* that further sharing is possible and potentially useful.

After my somewhat lame remark, there was quite a long silence, during which time Fran stopped crying and sat herself upright again. The silence was different from the embarrassed ones we'd sat through only a couple of weeks ago—it seemed somehow relaxed and quite intimate, and certainly gave us all time for reflection. Eventually, it was broken by Judy, not, I thought, because someone just *had* to say something, but because Judy felt she had something relevant to say: 'The number of times I've cried like that, Fran,' she began. Then she paused for a moment, thoughtfully, and added: 'Mind you, I've usually been alone when I have let go. I've never done it in public.' Fran replied, with a slight crack in her voice: 'I don't mind that. At least not with you. In fact, it even helps having you around.' Maggie nodded agreement, and Jenny added: 'Yes, this isn't really "public", is it?' (Community Home Girls' Group).

In addition to such cathartic emotional gains, however, there is that affective content of group experience, perhaps unexpressed and unexplored, which builds up to the point where tensions and often conflicts among group members become quite intense. The positive effects of such feelings can of course be enormous. At the very least they may sharpen key issues and so enable individuals, and the group as a whole, to define a clearer stance and to act more firmly and confidently on them. Such conflict may also clarify mutual expectations and perceptions, so that rigidities in relationships, and the points where these might be shifted, become more easily identifiable. The result may then be (as perhaps the Physically Handicapped Adolescent Group shows), that stated group goals are pursued more energetically, especially if the worker sees his functions within such conflict situations in a dynamic rather than a merely repressive way.

However, group tensions and conflicts do not always offer a target for constructive social work intervention. The Community Action Group is perhaps an example of how they can delay or even prevent group members becoming involved in both the instrumental tasks and the social transactions of the group. They can, for example, interfere seriously with communications in a group, so that information, opinions, attitudes and especially feelings are both transmitted and perceived in highly distorted forms. They can also produce considerable respondent behaviour which seriously displaces group goals from those which are ascribed, to ones concerned primarily with resolving the conflict. Thus, much genuinely disfunctional activity may appear as group members find themselves working mainly or entirely on establishing themselves in relation to others, no matter how exploitive they must be in the process. Instrumental activity may then become almost a secondary consideration, and some individuals may even leave the group altogether, long before it has begun to give them what they needed from it, and long before they have contributed to it as fully as they might have done.

The worker in such circumstances may then need to undertake either cathartic or suppressive functions, or even both. His target may indeed be the feelings of suspicion or hostility or anger which individuals have about each other. But his tactical objective may need to be not to build constructively on these feelings but primarily to release tension, again perhaps by doing rather than talking. Or he may himself need at times to block off the expression of the feelings which are proving so destructive, at least for the time being. And he may need to do this once more by emphasising —almost distracting group members with—the official task, and by throwing his own weight on to the side of those norms and roles which promise to stem the conflict. Perhaps this is what the worker in the Community Action Group was, rather intuitively, trying to do when he offered to intervene personally to get Mr Grey to meet the committee (p. 120).

To talk, as this chapter has done, of the worker's targets for intervention is undoubtedly to emphasise the worker's power, and also the importance of *his* perception of events rather than that of other group members. However, the reality is that, in a group, a social worker is for clients usually a highly 'significant other' whose contributions cannot but have a special importance. That is why, in this chapter, there has been one main underlying theme: the need for a worker in a group to maintain the maximum congruence between his intentions and both the *content* of his interventions and also their *form and manner*. Whether consciously this target is the practical and technical, cognitive, social or affective aspect of individuals' collective experience, the worker's deeds will invariably speak much more loudly than his words. They will therefore constitute the most significant examples of his intervention in the life of a group.

8

The future for group work

When the processes which occur in human groups are analysed, an impression may be created of intangible and confusing forces which no mere mortal could ever expect to understand, still less influence. And in reality, these processes are often complex, and, fortunately no doubt, do not lend themselves easily to manipulation. Just to hold one or two of the central concepts consciously in one's mind while one is actually immersed in practice, is therefore difficult enough. To internalise such concepts so that they are used appropriately yet unself-consciously is even more demanding, and can rarely be taken completely for granted.

Nonetheless, if this book leaves some uncertainty and lack of clarity, this must be the result, not only of the complexity of the processes themselves, but also of the limitations of the written word. Often, in fact, fine sounding phrases like 'intervening in group interaction' or 'using the group as a means as well as a context' merely describe behaviour which each of us performs every day. And certainly social workers, whose ascribed functions require them to work within a great variety of interpersonal situations, are—however intuitively—frequently acting out these abstract phrases all the time.

Some key assumptions

Precisely because so much of what is central to working in group situations is taken for granted, it seems worth restating in this final chapter the key assumptions on which this book rests.

1. *The pervasiveness of an interactionist perspective* First, it must be re-emphasised that, though many, often lengthy, passages may have suggested the contrary, it has been assumed throughout that a social worker does not operate as a group worker only in 'set-

piece' group situations. For, the interactionist perspective adopted here implies that, in each social encounter, individuals present themselves in some ways which are special to that encounter. Moreover, these situation-based presentations of self are affected continually both by the individual's self-image and self-expectations in such a situation, as well as by the expectations of others around them. As a result, the role-playing which results, to some degree *patterns* the individual's relationships with these others—that is, gives them a certain form and sets them within certain limits. As Ralph Ruddock (1969) puts it: 'role is the agency of relationship; that is to say, whenever we enter into a relationship, we adopt a role.'

Thus, for a social worker to be caught up in any experience of social exchange means that he will be faced with 'group work' demands. Even what he does, and looks for, as a caseworker can be very much affected by this point of view. For what the case-worker offers to the client in an interview is not a pure 'him'. He is not simply trying to build up a relationship between two constant and unchanging persons. In that interview, the worker offers his 'self-as-social worker', which is conditioned in significant ways by his own and the client's expectations of what such a self-presentation will comprise. He must accept, therefore, that the subsequent relationship is patterned—structured, moulded, pre-set within certain limits. No less important, what is offered in return by the individual he seeks to help is a 'self-as-client', as a 'helped person', as an 'interviewee'. Once again, the social context in which the encounter takes place and the client's and worker's expectations within it, stimulate certain types of role-playing by the client. And these, too, involve a patterning of the relationship between the two.

Thus, to act as group worker, a social worker does not necessarily have to bring certain individuals together formally into a group, or to enter an existing group situation which has a clear-cut form and boundaries. If he has developed any additional insights into human *interactions*, and any extra confidence and responsiveness when dealing with them, then he will have opportunities to apply these in every situation of interpersonal exchange.

2. *The importance of here and now relationships for the group worker* Second, and closely related to this, it seems worth re-stating explicitly that group work need not be identified solely with intensive psycho-therapeutic activity. Certainly, there may be periods in the lives of some individuals when this type of experience will be helpful—when they might confront themselves and each

other with feelings and motives normally lying hidden from public scrutiny.

This type of task is, however, by no means the only one on which, collectively, individuals might work. Nor is it even the only one which can provide therapy and growth in unsettled, unhappy, alienated or deprived lives. In the first place, we have now seen how 'the self' might to some extent be remade, at least in its specific presentation, in every social situation. Thus, *past* experience is clearly not the only determinant of current behaviour. Current experience and relationships can do much to form that behaviour; and at times, too, it can do much to shape current, and perhaps also, persisting attitudes, values and habits.

3. *The importance of the 'doing' and the 'being' as well as the 'saying' in group work* Third, this book has emphasised constantly that current experience is rarely if ever made up solely of what individuals *say* to each other, however probing these verbal exchanges may be. No less important at times is what they *do* together and to each other. And so, a social worker need not feel ashamed or inferior because he stimulates activity other than verbalisation, or because he looks on verbalisation simply as one element of a much broader range of human activity which he wishes to utilise. Individuals' non-verbal experiences of interacting can, in themselves, be positive and rewarding, as well as socially acceptable: they do not have to include deliberate articulation of the gains or of the processes producing those gains.

Moreover, it needs also to be recognised that 'doing' does not simply mean 'doing an activity'—discussing, rock-climbing, acting or whatever. Though such instrumental tasks are usually very influential within a group's experience, individuals' non-verbal impact on each other usually extends well beyond what the specific operations of such a task demands. The way these specific operations are carried out, the implicit as well as explicit values attached to such operations, the differential worth allocated to individuals performing different operations, the power-sharing which follows from this—in these and many other ways, group members (and group workers) involve themselves in highly significant forms of interpersonal 'doing'.

4. *The need for a generic methodology* Once again, then, we must draw the conclusion that 'group work' cannot be conceived simply as intervention by a social worker in a 'set-piece', activity-focused situation. And yet, it has to be admitted that for most practitioners today, such 'set-piece' approaches are in fact entirely synonymous

with 'doing group work', and the broader, more pervasive interactional perspective is given only limited, conscious application.

One effect of this has been to define group work as something
quite distinct from, and even in conflict with, other social work
methods, and especially casework. Such a definition is, however,
usually extremely inhibiting. And so, a fourth emphasis of this
book has been to regard group work as an integral part of a
generic social work method. Social workers, in other words, need to
feel able to move as required, and with a degree of personal comfort
and professional familiarity, between simple or complex interactional situations, and to apply a heightened understanding and
awareness to any of them. The more complex situations may again
be specially formed 'set piece' groups, or spontaneous or 'natural'
groups, or even fluid and perhaps larger 'community' groups. The
same body of knowledge, however, will remain appropriate.

It is true, of course, that a trend towards a *more varied* social
work methodology is now discernible in the field. However, this
is not in itself the same as a *generic* methodology, since any
individual worker is still liable to adopt only a single method—
that is, he is still liable to see himself, and to be seen by others, as
either a caseworker, *or* a group worker *or* community worker.
Practice that involves ready movement among two, or even all
three, methods by the same worker thus still remains rare. And so,
too, therefore, does the feeling (gained through actual experience)
that there may not even be three such distinct ways of working, but
simply different emphases in approach to different individuals in
different circumstances.

Moreover, many of the moves towards a more varied methodology which have occurred have been piecemeal. They have
depended often on the frustration, and the initiative, of individual
workers; or on the opportunist responses of particular agencies to
new challenges and demands; or on the often only half-thought-out
requirements of a new piece of legislation; or on the sudden upsurge
of a new idea which has become fashionable. This certainly would
seem to account for the popularity of much 'set-piece' group work
and of what is often labelled as 'community work'.

In themselves, however, these developments do not represent
any fundamental shift in the stance of the social work profession
as such. For the key assumptions of this book to become widely
accepted, major changes would have to occur in a number of
central philosophical and institutional areas of the profession. These
would certainly have to include:

(a) *The recruitment and selection of workers for the profession*
The publicity procedures and selection criteria which social work

at present adopts may well have to be modified so that the people recruited do not see themselves working solely or mainly with one individual at a time. It would of course be too simple, and at best not proven, to suggest that only certain 'personality types' are attracted to social work. Nonetheless, as long as social work portrays itself as largely synonymous with casework, it will almost certainly appeal primarily to those who wish to see themselves as caseworkers. It may even be that these recruits, by definition, find it difficult to imagine themselves working confidently with groups, so that a built-in bias in favour of one-to-one activity, and against group work, persists.

Yet, as other professions demonstrate, there is a pool of people very ready to expose themselves to group situations. Teaching is, of course, the prime example, though others, such as youth work and residential social work itself, are easily identifiable. And, given the size of the teaching profession in particular, these other professions almost certainly contain some who could just as easily have entered social work, and who might have done so if social work had not seemed so preoccupied with intensive one-to-one encounters.

Many other variables operate, of course, when individuals make decisions about their careers. And often some of these—like salary, status, and prospects—are enormously influential. Nonetheless, job content is important for many individuals, not least among those attracted to 'helping' activity. If social work's methods are to be diversified in any fundamental way, therefore, it may have deliberately to emphasise its concern with more than just one-to-one relationships.

(b) *Initial training* Already, many initial social work training courses include group work in their syllabuses and have made substantial gestures to a diversification of methods within the profession. However, the picture appears to be very patchy. Some—perhaps many—courses, still seem to concentrate their 'method' teaching almost exclusively on casework. Even where group work is included, its exact meaning and application can vary enormously. It may well have much less time allocated to it than casework. Supervised field experience may not be seen as essential to internalising whatever 'theory' is being taught, as it invariably would for casework. As a result, its priority for students may be very low; at best it may be regarded as an interesting excursion into some unusual, but not vital, territory. And certainly, few products of this training would be likely to internalise the type of pervasive interactionist perspective outlined in this book.

These remarks are written very largely with the field social

worker in mind. They may, however, apply also, in amended form, to the residential worker, whose need to develop this same perspective through pre-service training is, if anything, even more pressing.
(c) *In-service training* For the development of such a perspective, however, in-service training is probably even more critical than pre-service training. For, looked at in a purely statistical way, a major shift to a generic method which depends entirely on appropriately recruited and trained *new* entrants is unlikely to occur for two or even three generations.

However, in this case, the problem is not only a statistical one. For, even if *all* new entrants to social work were motivated and trained to act as group workers—an unlikely situation anyway—they would, for a long time to come, still constitute only a small minority of social work's total work force. They would thus constantly be subject to the enormously powerful pressures of 'institutional socialisation' which would almost certainly work mainly against major changes in method. Moreover, as new recruits, they would of course enter junior posts. They would then be subject to the influence, even control, of those in positions of power who have themselves been brought up in a completely different methodological tradition. To think, therefore, that a genuine shift of method will result simply because initial training has been modified—even assuming this is actually true—seems over-optimistic.

In other words, if the effects of initial training, even partially redirected, are to be felt and retained in the field, then the *re*-socialisation of many of those already working within the profession will have to occur very quickly. This implies a major effort at in-service training concentrated on social work method.

This will, of course, need to assume that many of those who participate already have substantial understanding of human motivation, behaviour and interaction. It will also have to recognise the expertise they already have in interpersonal situations, and to work through their current practice experience.

But it will also have to accept that these same people may have a deep emotional investment in a one-to-one approach. After all, this will have been the method in which originally they were trained—maybe, virtually indoctrinated—and/or on which they have relied almost exclusively as practitioners. 'Experts' in human relationships they may ostensibly be. This, however, will not necessarily make them immune from the caution and resistance to change to which human beings are prone when faced with unfamiliar demands and experience.

As a result, some clearly negative views about group work may be added to their unthinkingly positive emotional investment in casework. These, of course, may be rationalised as well as objectively justified. Yet their inhibiting effect on practice may be very great.

Undoubtedly, therefore, in-service training in group work will have to tackle attitudes and feelings, as well as to impart theory and concepts and to develop 'skills'. This, however, only seems to emphasise how substantial the in-service effort will need to be if it is to bring about the methodological shift advocated earlier. Not only would its size need to be enormous. So, too, would its intensity. At a time when even the teaching profession, with the much larger numbers involved, is beginning to offer its staff one term off every seven years for in-service training, can social workers—for this purpose as well as for many others—afford to do any less?

(d) *Content and methods of training for group work practice*

Realistically, of course, an effort on this scale is not very likely to occur. The resources it would require—time, money, teaching expertise, replacement staff for the field workers involved and so on—are almost certainly not going to be available. Nor probably, and even more crucially in the long run, is the will.

Thus, whatever training is provided (whether initial or in-service) will need to make the very most of its opportunities. On the precise form and content of this training, therefore, the social work profession will need to keep a very open mind—and probably a more open mind than it has done so far.

For, in so far as social work has involved itself in group work situations, it has been inclined, as we saw in Chapter 7, to identify itself, and especially in its training, very closely with T-group or sensitivity group approaches. Indeed, it has frequently been assumed—even by those who do not particularly approve of the idea—that training for work in groups must inevitably be of this kind, and that subsequent work with clients should use the same model.

However, it seems worth restating that one possible, and perhaps frequent, effect of this method could be to *reduce* participants' motivations actually to practise as group workers, by making them feel that their training group 'tutor' or 'consultant' so epitomised group work practice at its most skilful that they themselves could never even approach his or her level of skill.

In addition, social workers may have ethical doubts about this form of training. They may question the pressures it places on individuals, the stress it causes for them and the apparent lack of safeguards against serious and long-term damage. Again, such doubts may of course be rationalisations of personal fears and anxieties about an unknown or unfamiliar situation. Nonetheless, the outcome may be a refusal by those so affected to involve themselves in group work practice as they now conceive it.

This, of course, is not to accept uncritically socal workers' doubts about T-groups and similar methods. Nor is it to deny that such methods deserve an important place in social work training, not least because of their ability to stimulate personal growth and to increase self-awareness in the individuals taking part. (See for example, Ottoway, 1966). It is, however, to suggest, almost paradoxically, that the T-group as a means of training social workers (and perhaps others) for group work *practice* may be much more limited than is often acknowledged. And it is certainly to question whether an exclusive or even predominant use of this one method of group work training is really justified.

For, alternatives do exist. These too have their limitations, as do all the methods of training for the 'helping' professions currently in use. In particular, the transfer of learning from the point at which it is acquired theoretically, to the point at which it must be used in practice, remains difficult and extremely unreliable.

Nonetheless, the methods still regarded as appropriate for training in casework would seem to have at least as much justification in the context of group work training. The starting-point will clearly need still to be actual experience—that is, work in the field in group situations. Closely linked to this, will be opportunities to analyse what has been done, so that the practitioners can tease out the personal lessons of his experience, as well as the relevant learning on 'the theory of groups'. In this way, the mystique so often attached to group work may be removed, and meaningful courses in 'group dynamics' and 'group methods' introduced.

It is true, of course, that if a truly generic social work methodology is to emerge, such courses will still need to be integrated with whatever other 'methods' of teaching, particularly in casework and community work, are being offered. Nonetheless, developing more of this type of group work training will in itself represent an important first step away from social work's overwhelming identification with casework.

Such a training model is of course highly traditional and can hardly be said to have been an unqualified success even in the training of caseworkers. Certainly, as far as group work training is concerned, modifications may be essential. What constitutes a 'group situation', for example, will need to be more broadly and flexibly defined than 'the casework situation' normally is. As this book has repeatedly emphasised, it will not be enough to see this solely in terms of office-based discussion groups, as if it were sufficient simply to remake the casework interview in a new image. Informal as well as formal group encounters, outside the office (in the local neighbourhood, in other institutions and agencies, in the out-of-doors and so on) as well as within it will certainly need to be used.

Moreover, the balance may need to be shifted increasingly to experience, and away from extrapolated teaching of 'theory' in its own right. At the very least, the stress may need to be placed on teaching 'theory' which arises only or mainly out of controlled practice. Any training for human relations work must, of course, depend very heavily on such experience: because group work seems so often to bewilder social workers with its pace and confusion of events, training for it may demand an even greater emphasis of this sort, and so, even more than casework, may need to be rooted in the field and in field situations.

(e) *Recording* Such training, of course, assumes that students' analysis of their experience will be conducted in part through written description, interpretation and evaluation. However, for social workers, the 'recording' of group work may present problems. For, through their training as caseworkers, they may well have been brought up on 'process recording'—on recalling and re-presenting events as they occurred in as much detail as possible. The focus moreover may have been, not merely on *what* happened, but also on *how* it happened—on how events were linked together.

To record group encounters in this way is, however, almost impossible. Again, the speed and complexity of events make the casework analogy very inadequate. Too much happens to too many people too rapidly and in too many different ways. Thus one individual (the worker), who has himself had to continue to be involved in the action, can hardly expect to recall and re-present, in its proper order, everything that has occurred.

And yet a written analysis can be a vitally important tool of practical learning and self-development, as well as being an administrative requirement of the sponsoring agency. Two main ways of resolving the dilemma are available, though neither can be said to be ideal, and neither should be seen as excluding the other. First, the student group worker may attempt to record the process of one or two periods or passages of the total group experience. These may be defined solely in terms of time, and could even be quite arbitrarily laid down: say, the first five minutes of a meeting, or gathering, or the last five, or a set period in between. The events that occurred within these limits might indisputably have been crucial to much else that happened and so require detailed analysis. Or they might, on the contrary, not seem particularly critical, and therefore might deserve closer scrutiny precisely for this reason.

Selective process recording of this type is, then, one possible way of resolving the problem of gathering together and organising the mass of material which group work experience usually produces. Another response, however, might be to adopt a 'topical' approach to this experience. This means identifying certain facets of what has occurred, as potentially important, and then tracing them through the total encounter. Such landmarks might include, say, the worker's interventions and the targets at which they were directed (see Chapter 7); or the exercise of leadership or the incidence of exploitive behaviour within a group (see Chapter 5); or the interactiveness, or the rewards produced by the group's ascribed task (see Chapter 6).

This type of recording can often be systematised to some degree if the worker develops a check-list of key topics. This can then be applied to each group experience, so that he is made to focus on aspects of that experience which he might not otherwise have considered consciously. It might even become a record sheet, a recording form, which a worker completes after each group encounter.

Conclusion

The main message of this chapter is then simple and direct: work with groups (indeed, work in interactional situations generally) can undoubtedly contribute to social work practice. If it does no more than allow clients more varied channels of self-expression, and more diverse sources of information, practical and material help, and social and emotional support, the integration of such work with casework and community work seems amply justified.

However, if it is to be helpful to clients, such work will certainly have to be tackled with at least as much conviction, commitment and vigour as is casework at present. This will certainly mean that more resources—premises, equipment and money as well as people and their time and skill—will need to be allocated to it. But it will also—and, at first, probably more importantly—mean that recruitment and training procedures will have to be given some new and more varied emphases.

At the outset, this may well mean that social work in Britain has to pull itself up by its bootstraps. At present, it may lack many of the basic resources essential for a major shift towards a generic methodology, or even simply towards more frequent and disciplined use of groups. Such basic resources include opportunities for fieldwork practice, appropriate teaching materials, skilled and confident teachers and supervisors, and the endorsement (or even the mere tolerance) of group work by many superiors. Yet, if social workers do not actually begin to practise more often and in a more deliberate fashion in group situations, if they do not record and analyse these situations, if they do not include pre-service students in them, and act themselves, or force senior staff to act, as teachers of such students—if, that is, they do not proceed *as if* the resources already existed—then those resources will in fact never be created.

Over the last few years, this has in fact begun to happen at an increasing pace. Force of circumstances has, as we have seen, impelled many caseworkers into group work roles, and group work is now very much in fashion within the social work profession generally. For anything like a genuine diversification of methods to occur, however, this development will have to become much less piecemeal and also less opportunist. It will, in other words, need to establish its place within social work's total effort much more firmly, by being firmly and officially underpinned within training, field and residential institutions, and within the administrative machine.

Nonetheless, the fact that such developments are occurring is undoubtedly a cause for optimism. It means that the casework log-jam has at last been broken. An opportunity for developing social work's methods on a truly generic basis thus now exists. It may not recur for a very long time.

Suggestions for further reading

DOUGLAS, T., *A Decade of Small Group Theory*, Bookstall Publications, 1970.
KLEIN, A. F., *Social Work Through Group Process*, School of Social Welfare, State University of New York at Albany, USA, 1970.
RUDDOCK, R., *Roles and Relationships*, Routledge & Kegan Paul, 1969.
SCHWARTZ, W. and ZALBA, S. R. (eds), *The Practice of Group Work*, Columbia University Press, 1971.
VINTER, R. D. (ed.), *Readings in Group Work Practice*, Campus Publishers, Ann Arbor, USA, 1967.

Bibliography

ABERCROMBIE, M. L. J. (1960) *The Anatomy of Judgement*, Penguin.

APLIN, G. and BAMBER, R. (1973) 'Group work counselling', *Social Work Today*, vol. 3, no. 22.

ARGYLE, M. (1967) *The Psychology of Interpersonal Behaviour*, Penguin.

ARGYLE, M. (1972a) 'Working in groups', *New Society*, 26 October.

ARGYLE, M. (1972b), 'Group dynamics', *New Society*, 2 November.

ASHTON, E. T. (1972) 'Mirrors, masks and social workers', *Social Work Today*, vol. 3, no. 9.

BION, W. R. (1961) *Experiences in Groups*, Tavistock Publications.

BLAU, P. M. and SCOTT, W. R. (1963) *Formal Organisations: A Comparative Approach*, Routledge & Kegan Paul.

BRITISH ASSOCIATION OF SOCIAL WORKERS (1971) *Confidentiality in Social Work*, BASW.

BRITISH ASSOCIATION OF SOCIAL WORKERS (1972) *A Code of Ethics for Social Work*, BASW.

BROWN, J. A. C. (1954) *The Social Psychology of Industry*, Penguin.

BUTTON, L. (1967) *Some Experiments in Informal Group Work*, Dept of Education, University of Swansea.

BUTTON, L. (1969) *The Harbourgate Group*, Dept of Education, University of Swansea.

BUTTON, L. (1971) *Discovery and Experience*, Oxford University Press.

COMBS, A. W., AVILA, D. L. and PURKEY, W. W. (1971) *Helping Relationships: Basic Concepts for the Helping Professions*, Allyn & Bacon, Inc.

DAVIES, B. D. (1967) 'Jolt to U.S. social work', *New Society*, 25 May.

DAVIES, M. (1969) *Probationers in Their Social Environment*, HMSO.

DOUGLAS, T. (1970) *A Decade of Small Group Theory*, Bookstall Publications.

FOULKES, S. H. and ANTHONY, E. J. (1965) *Group Psychotherapy: The Psychoanalytic Approach*, Penguin.

GOETSCHIUS, G. W. and TASH, M. J. (1967) *Working With Unattached Youth*, Routledge & Kegan Paul.

GOFFMAN, E. (1959) *The Presentation of Self in Everyday Life*, Penguin.

GRAINGER, A. J. (1970) *The Bullring*, Pergamon Press.

GUMP, P. V. and SUTTON-SMITH, B. (1955) 'The "It" role in children's games', in *The Study of Games*, ed E. M. Avedon and B. Sutton-Smith, Wiley.

HARGREAVES, D. H. (1972) *Interpersonal Relations and Education*, Routledge & Kegan Paul.

HARTFORD, M. E. (1972) *Groups in Social Work*, Columbia University Press.

HOMANS, G. C. (1951) *The Human Group*, Routledge & Kegan Paul.

JORDAN, W. (1972) *The Social Worker in Family Situations*, Routledge & Kegan Paul.

KAYE, B. and ROGERS, I. (1968) *Group Work in Secondary Schools*, Oxford University Press.

KLEIN, A. F. (1970) *Social Work Through Group Process*, School of Social Welfare, State University of New York at Albany.

KONOPKA, G. (1972) *Social Group Work: A Helping Process*, Prentice-Hall, Inc.

MAIER, H. W. (1965) *Group Work as Part of Residential Treatment*, National Association of Social Workers (New York).

MATTHEWS, J. E. (1966) *Working With Youth Groups*, University of London Press.

MAYER, J. E. and TIMMS, N. (1970) *The Client Speaks*, Routledge & Kegan Paul.

MIDDLEMAN, R. R. (1968) *The Non-Verbal Method in Working with Groups*, Association Press.

MORSE, M. (1965) *The Unattached*, Penguin.

NORTHEN, H. (1969) *Social Work With Groups*, Columbia University Press.

OTTOWAY, A. K. C. (1966) *Learning Through Group Experience*, Routledge & Kegan Paul.

PHILLIPS, H. V. (1957) *Essentials of Group Work Skill*, Association Press.

RICE, A. K. (1965) *Learning for Leadership*, Tavistock Publications.

RICHARDSON, E. (1967) *Group Study for Teachers*, Routledge & Kegan Paul.

ROGERS, C. (1970) *On Encounter Groups*, Penguin.

RUDDOCK, R. (1969) *Roles and Relationships*, Routledge & Kegan Paul.

SARRI, R. C. and GALINSKY, M. J. (1967) 'A conceptual framework for group development', in *Readings in Group Work Practice*, ed. R. D. Vinter, Campus Publishers, Ann Arbor.

SCHWARTZ, W. (1961) 'The social worker in the group', in *New Perspectives on Services to Groups*, National Association of Social Workers (New York).

SCHWARTZ, W. (1966) 'Neighborhood centres', in *Five Fields of Social Service*, ed. H. S. Maas, National Association of Social Workers (New York).

SCHWARTZ, W. (1971) 'Neighborhood centres and group work', in *Research in the Social Services*, ed. H. S. Maas, National Association of Social Workers (New York).

SCHWARTZ, W. and ZALBA, S. R. (eds) (1971) *The Practice of Group Work*, Columbia University Press.

SHULMAN, L. (1971) 'Program in group work: another look', in *The Practice of Group Work*, ed. W. Schwartz and S. R. Zalba, Columbia University Press.

SMITH, C. S., FARRANT, M. R. and MARCHANT, H. J. (1972) *The Wincroft Youth Project*, Tavistock Publications.

SMITH, G. (1970) *Social Work and the Sociology of Organisations*, Routledge & Kegan Paul.

SOMERS, M. L. (1968) 'The small group in learning and teaching' in *Education for Social Work*, ed. E. Younghusband, George Allen & Unwin.

STURTON, S. (1972) 'Developing groupwork in a casework agency', *British Journal of Social Work*, vol. 2, no. 2.

SUTTON-SMITH, B. (1955) 'The psychology of children's games', *National Education* (New Zealand), vol. 37.

THORPE, D. (1973) 'Working with young people', *Social Work Today*, vol. 3, no. 23.

THORPE, D. (1973) 'Three kinds of intermediate treatment', *Social Work Today*, vol. 3, no. 24.

THORPE, D. (1973) 'The shape of intermediate treatment', *Social Work Today*, vol. 3, no. 25.

TROPP, E. (1968) 'The group: in life and in social work', *Social Casework* (US), May.

VINTER, R. D. (1959) 'Group work: perspectives and prospects', in *Social Work with Groups, 1959*, National Association of Social Workers (New York).

VINTER, R. D. (1961) 'New evidence for restructuring group services', in *New Perspectives on Services to Groups*, National Association of Social Workers (New York).

VINTER, R. D. (1967a) 'The essential components of social group work practice', in *Readings in Group Work Practice*, ed. R. D. Vinter, Campus Publishers, Ann Arbor.

VINTER, R. D. (1967b) 'Program activities: an analysis of their effects on participant behavior', in *Readings in Group Work Practice*, ed. R. D. Vinter, Campus Publishers, Ann Arbor.

VINTER, R. D. (ed.) (1967c) 'An approach to group work practice', *Readings in Group Work Practice*, Campus Publishers, Ann Arbor.

YOUNGHUSBAND, E. (1973) 'The future of social work', *Social Work Today*, vol. 4, no. 2.